CREEPY
FLORIDA

Phantom Pirates, the Hog Island Witch,
the Demented Doctor at the Don Vicente & More

MARK MUNCY AND KARI SCHULTZ

THE
History
PRESS

Published by The History Press
Charleston, SC
www.historypress.com

Copyright © 2019 by Mark Muncy and Kari Schultz
All rights reserved

Cover illustration by Kari Schultz

First published 2019

Manufactured in the United States

ISBN 9781467142007

Library of Congress Control Number: 2019943378

CONTENTS

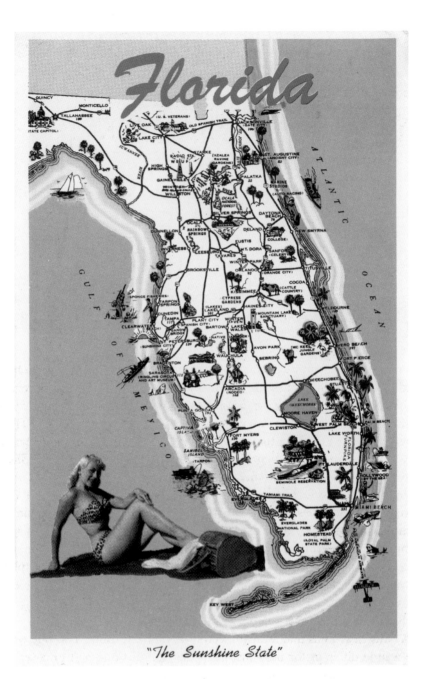

Florida—The Sunshine State. 1959. Color postcard, fourteen by nine centimeters.
Courtesy of State Archives of Florida, Florida Memory.

INTRODUCTION

Greetings, traveler.

You hold in your hands our third book from The History Press. Kari Schultz and I have worked on these three books for the last four years. Our previous books, *Eerie Florida* and *Freaky Florida*, explored the monsters, myths and legends that lurk on the dark side of the Sunshine State. From the UFO flaps in Gulf Breeze to Robert the Haunted Doll in Key West, we did our best to cover some famous and forgotten legends to give our readers the ultimate travel guide for something other than just beaches and theme parks.

While we were working on our previous books, we traveled more than seven thousand miles without leaving the state. We'd been Squatchin' on Skunk Ape Hunts. We'd looked for sea and river monsters. We'd even spent some time in nearly every museum, historical archive and library in the state. At every stop in every town, we discovered more and more legends to explore. It seems that we will never be able to chase down every legend this amazing state has to offer. What really stood out to us in all of our adventures was one major point: nearly every place we went had a ghost story.

It was clear to us that a third volume would be in order. This one would be a little different for us. Kari and I decided this one had to cover one thing we had kept to a minimum in the other books. This book would be completely about hauntings.

When you speak of haunted Florida houses, there are a few names that seem to rise to the top of any "most haunted" list. While we certainly intend to touch on some of the most famous cases in this book, we'd also like to focus on some of the lesser-known haunts. We visited the Cuban Club in our second book, *Freaky Florida*. The ghosts there supposedly number in the hundreds, and no one is really sure how many deaths are tied to the building. We also discussed many of the ghosts of St. Augustine for our first book, *Eerie Florida*. I'm not saying we've saved the best for last, but we purposely held on to many ghost stories just in case this book came to fruition. Be sure to pick through those older books for some other great ghostly tales.

Something else we noticed when looking into the stories was that the ghosts in the stories were always the most famous people associated with the locations of the haunts. I'm not sure if this was just a way to make the haunting less scary or to make the place seem more important. While there is some evidence of Al Capone frequently visiting Tampa Bay, how likely is it that he has decided to haunt a building he "may have" spent some nights in? Babe Ruth and Teddy Roosevelt are also common ghosts. Jack Kerouac, Ernest Hemingway and even some Hollywood celebrities supposedly have spectral apparitions here in the Sunshine State. We went into several places with celebrity ghosts with more than a little pinch of salt. While we were frequently told the "celebrity story," we found other more likely candidates for the hauntings just as often.

If you followed our previous books, you know that we try to map them from north to south. That way you can use the book as a roadmap of sorts if you want to follow in our footsteps. This book is no different. While some locations are more famous or have a higher "fear factor" than others, we decided that people would want to use this as a travel guide to go with our other books. We love to see our dedicated fans on the "Eerie Florida Fans" Facebook page chronicle their own visits to the locations in our books.

Many of the haunted places detailed within the pages of this book are on private property. Even more have specific visitation hours. We would like to take a moment to remind legend-trippers and amateur ghost hunters to make sure you obey the law and do not trespass. Do not damage any private or public property you visit. Make sure you contact owners and caretakers ahead of time. Many are thrilled to talk to visitors about their own ghostly experiences. If you can't get into a closed location at three o'clock in the morning on the day you want to, just don't go. You might get arrested or worse—accidentally wind up becoming a ghost yourself.

One tip is to try to team up with local amateur, professional or enthusiast paranormal investigation groups. Many of them have established relationships with the more famous locations nearby. A fair number of groups host public events for fundraising efforts, which can be a great way to get to know if a group has the right fit for you.

For those of you who read our previous books and know all about us, you can skip the next two paragraphs after we give you a hearty "Thank you" for supporting our work. For those of you just joining us, you've got a couple of options. You can go out and get *Eerie Florida* or *Freaky Florida* and read them. We'll wait. Or, I can give you our credentials and a bit of our own history now. Still here? Then read on.

I'm Mark Muncy, an actor and historian who owned and operated a charity haunted house attraction in St. Petersburg, Florida, called Hellview Cemetery, for twenty years. We based the attraction on local lore and legends to give the Halloween event its own spin. We collected stories and legends for years, and we turned those into spooky tales on our website. Eventually my co-author, Elizabeth Abbott, and I collected those tales into books of their own, including *31 Tales of Hellview Cemetery* and *Tales of Terror of Tampa Bay*. After Hellview was closed by the city for being a little too successful, we were left with a load of legends that needed sharing.

I teamed up with illustrator and photographer Kari Schultz, and we hit the road. Some stories led to dead ends, but many led to unexpected conclusions. We tried to go straight to the source of all of the legends and ghost stories and tied them to the history of the area to give the stories a frame of reference. For those monsters or spirits that wouldn't pose for anything other than blurry photos, Kari brought them to life as detailed sketches.

Now that we're all caught up, there's just a little more to let you know what you are in for in this book. While in the previous books we explained the areas and history in as much detail as we felt necessary to explain the context of the legend, ghostly tales tend to lend themselves to open interpretation. While the history is still included where needed, some of these tales are mired in mystery. We did our best to explain the details of each haunting as we heard it and pointed out multiple narratives of each event if we felt they were appropriate or even known. It seems that some of the ghostly tales tend to get even more twisted than some of our most twisted legends we researched in the past.

We stand on the shoulders of giants who came before us. Charlie Carlson, Owl Goingback, Brandy Stark and many more have all explored the myths, monsters and legends of Florida before us. We are happy to update their findings with our own humble additions.

We must thank quite a few people for this book. Mostly, we have to thank Elizabeth Abbott for her early, and final, edits and for joining us on our crazy adventures as she continues to research her own projects. We must also thank our volunteer editing squad of Vanya Glyr, Dani Cervantes and Ken Barr—we couldn't have done it without you. We also have to acknowledge the wonderful team at The History Press for continuing to support us. Jonny Foster, Joe Gartrell, Crystal Murray and Hayley Behal are an amazing team that has our back.

The path for this book begins in northwest Florida, in the panhandle, and proceeds to the northeastern border of the state. From there, the path zigzags east to west as we travel south—all the way to the southernmost point in the United States in Key West. Follow the contents, and you can probably figure out the roads we took. Kari has posted an "Eerie Florida Travel Guide" on GoogleMaps™ that you can access at eerieflorida.com. Feel free to use that to find locations to plan some outings. It is updated frequently as we continue our journeys to discover even more monsters, ghosts, myths and legends.

We have a lot of places to cover in this book and only so much space and, for the first time, a wonderful full-color insert! Kari had her hands full with photography and photo editing, so I'm afraid fans of her art might be a little disappointed with the limited number of sketches in this book. I hope that her third knockout cover design and the occasional drawing will pique your interest. If you want more of her art, pick up *Eerie Alabama*, also from The History Press, which also kept her busy this year.

To keep up with us and maybe meet Kari and me, you can find our appearance schedule at eerieflorida.com. You can also follow us on most social media by looking for @eerieflorida. Our YouTube channel has a large number of videos from our travels and some of our television appearances. If you would like us to appear at your friendly local bookstore, event, convention, library or whatever, make sure to contact us through our website, so we can try to make that happen.

As always, I only feel it is proper to tell you that I present these stories with a friendly warning. You may find some of the stories disturbing. You may find them frightening. Some of them may even horrify you. So, if you feel you are of a delicate disposition, well…don't say I didn't warn you.

See you on the other side!

—Mark Muncy

PENSACOLA

Pensacola is the westernmost city in the Florida Panhandle. The first United States Naval Air Station was founded in Pensacola, and it is still the base of operations for the world-famous Blue Angels squadron. The city is a thriving port town known for its white sand beaches on the Gulf of Mexico. The town gets its name from the early native inhabitants of the area known as the Pensacola of the Muskogean language people. Many call the city the western gateway to the Sunshine State.

When the Spanish first tried to colonize the area in 1559, they were hit by a massive hurricane. They fled deep into what is now Alabama. After even more hardships returning to the coast, they decided that the land they referred to as *La Florida* had a line of safety much farther south. They left and avoided North Florida for 137 years.

The city is frequently referred to as the "City of Five Flags," referring to the five different countries that laid claim to it over the years. The Spanish, the French, the British, the U.S. and, of course, the Confederate flag during the Civil War have all flown over the area of Pensacola. With so much history, is there any doubt that there are ghost stories aplenty?

Madam Mollie McCoy presided over a famous bordello during the late nineteenth and early twentieth centuries. Mollie's bordello was a highly regarded establishment in the heart of Pensacola's thriving red-light district. Her brothel catered to an elite clientele, many of whom were naval officers, politicians and prominent businessmen. Pensacola was booming at this time, and the growth of the port created a unique economic and social environment.

Mollie McCoy's Boarding House was located at 15 Zaragossa Street. Her name was displayed proudly in gilt letters inscribed in the glass of the front door. The house was opulently furnished and was always spotless. Mollie took pride in her house.

The madam also took pride in her girls. She handpicked her girls and gave them strict rules to follow. In return for not drinking or smoking in public, she gave them fine gowns and classes in manners and elocution. The girls could only walk in groups outside the house and must never be alone. Any unladylike behavior would be met with expulsion from the house.

The city generally turned a blind eye to Mollie's illegal business. They felt it was a necessary evil that helped maintain order and reduce lawlessness. There were many gambling dens and bars along the harbor, so Mollie's area became a nice buffer area before returning to normal society.

When Mollie died in 1920, the house closed. It later became the Liberty Hotel, then the headquarters for the Waterfront Rescue Mission. It was finally demolished in 1966.

Since the 1940s, people have often reported seeing groups of women walking along Zaragossa Street. Usually in groups of three, these spectral women are often described as wearing Victorian or turn-of-the-century dress. They avoid contact with others and will even race across the street to avoid getting too close. Mollie is buried at St. John's Cemetery, but her spirit is often reported to be seen walking arm-in-arm with an invisible paramour along Zaragossa. One paranormal investigation group asked her who she was often seen walking with and received an Electronic Voice Phenomena (EVP) recording with the answer, "I walk with death."

These apparitions are usually seen just across from the Quayside Art Gallery, which has also had many ghostly incidents that are most likely connected to previous inhabitants of the old building. Visitors to the former firehouse have reported seeing shadowy figures and hearing disembodied voices. One particularly scary encounter involved an employee, who heard what she insisted was a body being dragged across the floor above late one evening. She was on the top floor, and the floor above had been demolished many years before.

Across Jefferson Street from the gallery lies the Pensacola Cultural Center. This building was once the Escambia County Court of Record building. It was built in 1911 and stayed in operation until the late 1970s. It housed a jail and courtrooms in addition to being used as a general-use courthouse for the booming city. Most notably, it held built-in gallows on the third floor. This execution room was used more often than one might think.

Many hauntings are reported here, including a small child who giggles and hides when sought. No one is quite sure who she is, but she is known to linger for those who bring her treats. There are dark shadows and deep cold spots that seem to be former prisoners who met their ends in the execution room. One is reported to be Hosea Poole, who was convicted of killing his brother and was executed on July 31, 1920. He was the last person executed here, but his ghost still wanders the halls of the Cultural Center.

A short distance away lies St. Michael's Cemetery. This eight-acre cemetery lies near the heart of the city of Pensacola. Though records show it was used by the Spanish in the mid- to late eighteenth century, the earliest surviving marker dates to 1812. There are more than three thousand marked graves and more than four thousand suspected unmarked graves.

Many prominent members of the city are buried here, including William Blount and Don Francisco Moreno. Moreno built the first bank in the city and was often referred to as the "King of Pensacola" due to his high ranking with the fledgling United States government and his status with the Spanish. Blount was a prominent attorney and head of the American Bar Association for a time.

The cemetery is the second oldest in Florida, so of course, it is home to many ghost stories. The most striking story involves sailors who were on leave during World War II. They walked by the graveyard, looking for a way to release some steam from being cooped up at sea. According to their accounts, a large, glowing skeleton rose from one of the graves and charged at one of the sailors. When the skeleton touched his skin, it blistered. They ran away, and when they reported back to duty, they were quarantined immediately. They had all been diagnosed with yellow fever, though the sailors had all been inoculated against it. Hallucination or not, yellow fever was a common killer in early Florida, and many who are buried at St. Michael's Cemetery were victims.

To this day, there are reports of strange lights and voices among the tombstones. Ghost hunters frequent the area due to the sheer number of graves and sightings. Most recent reports involve a man in dress from the 1920s walking the interior perimeter of the cemetery.

Captain William Northrup built a house on West Gregory Street. It is now the Victorian Inn Bed and Breakfast, and visitors and employees have often heard strange and unusual sounds in the inn. Piano music is often heard as well as the patter of children running through the halls. Most famously, the smell of cooked bacon and eggs emanates from the kitchen even before the chefs have begun operation for the guests. A spectral lady in white is often seen inside and sometimes even through the windows by those passing by.

The historic Seville Quarter was once the Pensacola Cigar and Tobacco Company warehouse. A musician and ex-navy pilot, Bob Snow, decided to rent the old warehouse and restore it to make a club for his band. It was a smash hit, and Snow expanded into the rest of the warehouse with other businesses. Rosie O'Grady's Goodtime Emporium specialized in spirits, food and Dixieland jazz. Snow later went on to replicate his success with the famous Church Street Station in Orlando.

The building is haunted by Wesley, a former bartender at Rosie's. Legend has it that he died of hypothermia after hitting his head in the walk-in freezer. He is frequently cited as the cause of numerous poltergeist-like activities at the bar, including thrown glasses and employees finding chairs moved into strange arrangements at opening. There are incident reports of him flirting with attractive female patrons and then inappropriately touching them on their posteriors. When the accosted try to remove his hand or slap him, he vanishes.

Mind your manners when you visit the Dorr House on Seville Square in Pensacola. The ghosts here are known to be violent to those who are rude or disrespectful. *Courtesy of author.*

Another spirit of the building is known as Sarah. She and her husband were in an older building that stood on the warehouse site when the city was attacked by pirates. The pirates killed her husband and attacked her. She managed to gouge out one of the pirate's eyes, and they decapitated her. Her headless ghost is often seen walking the upstairs office area of Seville Quarter or on the road out front.

Seville Square was once a Spanish outpost named San Miguel. It was made into a public square by the British and remains a public park to this day. Many great places to eat border the square, and there are often weddings and festivals within the park. This one block in Pensacola holds many haunted locations. Nearly every building on the square has spirits with stories to tell.

The most notable ghostly location on this block is the Dorr House. This house is currently owned by the University of West Florida and houses its president. It is frequently opened for tours and is beautifully furnished with many antiques.

The mirror in the sitting room area is said to have the strangest manifestations. If a ghost-sensitive woman stares into the mirror for a long period of time, a strong smell of roses will arise. She will also often feel a tugging sensation from behind. The crying of a female voice is also commonly heard echoing from upstairs. During one ghostly encounter at the house, a visitor who was using adult language and being very rude was shoved to the ground by an unseen hand. Mind your manners at this haunted building!

Just down the street on the square is the Old Christ Church. Three ghostly spirits have been seen marching through the pews in broad daylight. One will stop to pray at the altar before they all disappear into thin air. Many believe them to be the three vicars reburied in the church after it was built. There have been many witnesses to these sightings, so it is difficult for the church to try to keep it out of public knowledge, but they do not like to talk about it.

Across the plaza lies the Gray House, which is haunted by Captain Thomas Moristo, a sailor from the eighteenth century. His ghost is often seen through the windows of the building when it is unoccupied. Many investigations have taken place in the house with hit-or-miss results. The smell of cigars is often noted as a sign that the captain is walking the halls again.

Most ghost tours in the area will include the following famous haunted locations. The Pensacola Lighthouse is notably haunted by a murdered

The Old Christ Church is supposedly home to several ghostly former abbots of the church. *Courtesy of author.*

lighthouse keeper and a woman named Ella who died during childbirth. The nearby Naval Station is the home of a ghostly retired Marine Corps Ace named Captain Guy Hall, who died in a training mission. A former commodore has also been seen walking the halls after dying of the dreaded yellow fever. Fort Pickens, which we discussed in *Freaky Florida*, was the prison for Geronimo and many of his people. There have been numerous sightings of Native American spirits walking around the ruined fort.

THE PANHANDLE

Fort Walton Beach, Destin and Ocheesee

The Florida Panhandle is a vague area stretching about two hundred miles westward from the peninsula and bordered by Alabama, Georgia and the Gulf of Mexico. This northwestern arm of Florida is home to little, quaint beach towns and huge, sprawling tourist areas. Farther inland, small towns, dense swamps and old Florida forests lie just off the highways and main boulevards.

The Magnolia Grill was once a catalogue home purchased from Sears. Doctor G.G. French had the materials for the house shipped in 1910. It had a kitchen, a bathroom and several bedrooms in a two-story frame. It is now owned by Tom and Peggy Rice and houses a museum and an amazing restaurant. It also houses some great ghost stories.

The home is known for the ghost of a little old lady who lived there when it was a boardinghouse. She is still seen wandering the restaurant and often interacts with guests and staff. Tom and Peggy bought the house in 1998, and though they haven't seen her personally, there are stories among the staff of her even helping with the dishes.

When the home was a boardinghouse, an artist named Sandoval stayed for a time to paint the beaches and other serene sights near the town of Fort Walton Beach. After a particularly beautiful piece was completed, Sandoval locked himself in his room and began to deface his own art. He painted a blood-red rabbit over his painting, then continued to do this with several of his other paintings. He later swore that he had been possessed and had been forced to paint the floppy-eared rabbits all over his own work. He fled and never returned to Florida.

The Magnolia Grill (also known as the French House) in Fort Walton Beach was a kit home ordered and built from a Sears catalogue. It is now a wonderful restaurant. *Courtesy of author.*

The picture of the girls who like to change position at night at the Magnolia Grill. *Courtesy of author.*

Tom Rice recently brought a painting of two of his aunts who died in childbirth from his home in Xenia, Ohio. The painting was placed in the hallway at the foot of the stairs. The two girls pictured are often seen swapping places in the painting. Ghostly children's laughter is heard in the hallway as well. Tom and Peggy aren't sure if the painting itself was haunted before they brought it to the Magnolia Grill or if it is a result of the house. Either way, make sure to stop by the restaurant for amazing culinary delights and a little history while you are visiting. Tom's World War II artifact collection in the attic is particularly impressive. But keep your eyes open for the many ghostly inhabitants of the French House.

The Brooks Bridge is home to a controversial haunting. Connecting Fort Walton Beach and Okaloosa Island, US 98 crosses over this bridge. It was built in 1965 to replace an old 1930s steel span bridge, and thousands of vehicles cross it daily. The ghosts sighted here are highly unusual, as they only appear at specific times each month. At midnight on Wednesday nights, a spectral pack of wolves can be seen racing along the shore toward the bridge. When they near the bridge, the pack curves out and continues to run on top of the water. Witnesses claim they have an eerie glow about them. Some witnesses say that if they make eye contact with you, an uncanny sense of cold moves through you. Once the pack races under the bridge, they vanish.

We went to see this and were surprised to see others lined up along the bridge hoping to see the ghostly wolves. The legend was much more well-known than we anticipated. Some of the people we spoke with told us it only happens on the third Wednesday of the month, while others insisted it was only the first Wednesday after a full moon. A final person said we were all wrong, and it was the Destin Bridge near Crab Island on the other side of Okaloosa Island where the pack is seen more often. We investigated this location as well and saw no wolves ourselves, but far fewer people were convinced that was the location of the ghost wolves.

One of the watchers claimed to have seen the wolves on a few occasions. He said there are always at least three and sometimes as many as a dozen. He shivered when he spoke of looking down and making eye contact with the lead wolf as it passed under the bridge. He wanted to see it again as he felt that he made a connection with the spectral hound.

There are some other strange stories following along the I-10 corridor, and the following is one of the strangest stories we've ever investigated. The Ocheesee Pond in North Florida is famous for good fishing and lots of animal life. At one point, the town of Ocheesee was a boomtown and a stop on the stagecoach line from the capital in Tallahassee to the ports at Pensacola. The town was also a big part of the early turpentine industry in Florida until something started harassing the populace.

The pack of spectral wolves of Brooks Bridge make their run by moonlight. *Illustration by Kari Schultz.*

The Ocheesee Pond has many swampy areas around its edges. A glowing green figure is frequently reported in these areas. *Courtesy of author.*

The lack of small game was first noted by the local trappers. Then came small thefts of food that was left outside for too long, which escalated into farm animals being massacred. Fearing restless Native Americans or outlaws, a posse was formed to search the area around the pond to see if they could find the culprit. The posse returned with a capture no one expected. It was a wild man—a giant who stood at least seven feet tall, according to some reports. The man was covered in hair and was barely able to pass as human. The posse had come upon him and shot him in the leg, and when they brought him in, he was put in a cage. He reportedly smelled so foul that everyone kept their distance from the cage.

Not knowing what to do with this captive, the town decided to attach the cage to the next stagecoach headed for Tallahassee and let the governor deal with it. The arrival of the Wild Man of Ocheesee Pond made sensational headlines in the capital. Still not sure he was even human, they shipped him off to the state mental institution. After that, the wild man's fate is unknown.

Some say this was the first recorded capture of a Florida Skunk Ape, or Sasquatch. Some believe it was just some poor madman living in the swamps. All that is known is that he was shaved at the mental hospital, but there are no records beyond those initial reports of the Wild Man's arrival.

Those who live in the remote area around Ocheesee Pond say they sometimes see a large, glowing green shape marching along the shoreline.

The ghost of the Wild Man of Ocheesee Pond is still seen in the swampy lands around the pond. *Illustration by Kari Schultz.*

Others say the smell of death and decay precedes the sighting of the glowing, giant, hairy creature. Could this be the ghost of the Ocheesee Wild Man?

A short distance away in the town of Two Egg, Florida, they already have a mini-Bigfoot creature called the Two Egg Stump Jumper. This beast is shorter than five feet and moves like lightning. He is often seen on tree stumps and moves so fast that he seems to teleport. His movements and appearance are so jarring that some have theorized that he, too, is the ghost of a Skunk Ape.

Ghostly Bigfoots? If you travel the backroads through the Florida Panhandle, be sure to keep your eyes peeled.

MARIANNA

The town of Marianna is right in the heart of the panhandle. It is a picturesque Florida town with beautiful manor homes that was founded in 1838 by Scottish businessman Scott Beverage. He named the town after his daughters Mary and Anna, and the town became the seat for Jackson County shortly thereafter. Its official nickname is the "City of Southern Charm," and it still lives up to it today.

The Russ House is one of the most iconic buildings in the city. It was built in 1895 by Joseph W. Russ Jr. The Russ family had extensive landholdings in Marianna, and their home was to be built at the site of a famous Civil War battle that was fought more than thirty years prior. The house was owned and occupied by the Russ family for exactly one hundred years.

With the stock market crash of 1929, the Russ family was forced to sell most of its land. They began to offer the house as a place to host events and galas for a small fee. They did everything they could to maintain the house. In 1930, in a fit of despondency over the loss of the family fortune, Joseph W. Russ Jr. killed himself in the house. With this tragic event, the haunted reputation of the Russ House began, though many claim it was never truly empty of spirits, implying that the spirits of those who died in the Civil War battle also occupied it.

During World War II, the family rented the upstairs rooms to officers from the nearby base. They continued to host functions for the city, and the house was repeatedly mortgaged to help finance the lives of the Russ family and maintain their home. The house fell into disrepair through the late 1980s

The Russ House is considered by many to be the most photographed haunted house in Florida because it is so picturesque. Photographers often realize there are figures staring out of the windows in their shots. *Courtesy of author.*

and early 1990s. In 1995 the house was sold to the City of Marianna and was restored by 2000. It is now home to the Jackson County Chamber of Commerce and is open to the public. The house is also available to be rented for weddings, events and even overnight ghost hunts. Because the house is so iconic, it is frequently photographed, which has brought to light many ghostly images staring out of the windows and on the grounds. Many say it is the most photographed haunted house in Florida.

Decades before the building of the Russ House, Marianna was the home of Governor John Milton, an ardent secessionist during the Civil War. He made the town into one of the largest cities in North Florida under Confederate control in 1864. It was an important supply station and mustering center for militia before they would head off to fight farther north.

This made the town a prime target for the Union forces that controlled nearby Pensacola. On the morning of September 27, a seven-hundred-deep column of soldiers on horseback led by Union brigadier general Alexander Asboth approached the outskirts of Marianna. Confederate colonel Alexander B. Montgomery oversaw the defense of the area. He had spread his forces thin to try to figure out where the Union forces were attempting to go. It wasn't until Asboth reached Marianna that Montgomery knew for certain what their target was.

The Confederate colonel pulled up the area's home guard and the reserves he could find. He set up an ambush point along what is now West Layfette Street. The Confederate skirmishers met the charging Union forces at a place called Hopkins' Branch, which was just outside of town, before withdrawing down the main road. Montgomery's own cavalry fled down a bypass road to try to approach behind the barricades. The Union's commander split his forces as well, and some went down the same bypass to try to flank the town. Both armies were committed.

Asboth led a charge down the main street right into the barricaded street. He realized too late that an ambush was awaiting his troops, and a volley of fire came from the home guard soldiers stationed at the ambush site. Many senior officers died in the initial attack, and Asboth's face was wounded. The sheer number of Union troops were eventually able to push past the barricade and into the town. The battle continued, and the flanking Union forces were able to drive away Montgomery's cavalry and even captured the colonel as he attempted to flee.

In town, the fighting of the defenders continued, and many fled to St. Luke's Episcopal Church. A regiment of United States Colored Troops

St. Luke's Episcopal Church in Marianna was where the Battle of Marianna culminated. *Courtesy of author.*

engaged those in the church. The fighting continued until the Union used a bayonet charge to capture the bulk of the forces. Some snipers were still firing from the church and refusing to surrender.

The Union forces set fire to the church and began to shoot the fleeing Confederates. According to one account, the pastor ran into the burning church to save the Bible within. All in all, ten Confederates were slain and sixteen were wounded. Fifty-four prisoners were captured, but thirteen were released because they were locals defending their homes. Of the Union forces, eight were killed, nineteen were wounded and ten were captured. General Asboth's facial wound never properly healed. He died of complications from the wound a few years later in 1868.

With so many casualties, especially among high-ranking officers, the Union forces returned to Pensacola with many freed slaves, tons of looted food stores, cattle and horses. The area would not fully recover from the devastation for years.

St. Luke's basement is said to host the ghost of a Confederate soldier, who appears in rags and stinks of smoke. Another ghost is said to be a flaming spirit that bursts out of the side door and runs to a nearby grave before vanishing. Another spirit in the building has been witnessed being overprotective of the Bible on the altar. A Union soldier whose eye was shot out by a Confederate sniper in the church is said to wander the surrounding graveyard. The whole area around downtown Marianna is littered with spirits from this battle.

For more than a century, the story of the ghost of the Bellamy Bridge has been one of the most famous haunted tales ever told. The legend states that young Elizabeth Bellamy had just been married when her dress caught fire. She fled the wedding screaming and ran to the nearby Chipola River to drown out the flames. She lived for two more days in unending agony before succumbing to her horrific wounds. Her young husband killed himself shortly thereafter. Her ghost is seen marching along the banks of the river near the Bellamy Bridge in a gown made of fire.

Is it true? No.

Elizabeth Croom married Samuel Bellamy in North Carolina. She not only survived the wedding but also moved to Florida with her husband and young son. The dreaded yellow fever struck the young woman, and she was buried near the site of the Bellamy Bridge. Her son died a week later and was buried beside her. Her husband followed them into the afterlife many years later.

The story of the fiery dress and young bride derives from a story in a novel by eighteenth-century author Caroline Lee Hentz, a native of nearby Marianna. She told the tale of a slave bride who was married in a big house on the Bellamy Plantation. Her books were often said to be based on true events, so many began to associate her book with the Bellamy Bridge. Caroline is buried at the cemetery at St. Luke's Episcopal Church.

Another ghostly tale tells of a headless horseman who rides along the old trail toward the Bellamy Bridge. He is covered in flames, and his horse has flaming hooves. Variants of this story say that he is headless but has no flames until he draws a blade. One telling of the story claims that the horseman was a Spanish soldier fleeing Native Americans who shot him with flaming arrows. The Spanish did use this area as a crossing, and the native people of the area also used it as a natural ford for the Chipola River. The bridge was built sometime in 1914—long after poor Elizabeth Bellamy had passed away. Could it be her ghost wandering the banks of the river looking for her son? Could the horseman be some other story we've yet to unearth that ties into the mysterious flaming lady in white fire? We may never know for certain.

What we do know is that we recommend bringing plenty of mosquito repellant, as this area is a hotbed for the beasts. The bugs explain many of the "orbs" caught on camera at the site. The full-bodied apparitions, however, are another thing entirely.

For those unfamiliar with Dozier, the Florida School for Boys opened in 1900 and stayed open until 2011. The school was meant to house one

The Dozier School Church is the only part of the infamous school that is not fenced in. The sounds of singing and boys playing can often be heard here, though it has been out of use since 2010. *Courtesy of author.*

hundred of the worst juvenile criminals in the Florida legal system. It did not take long for the roster to inflate to more than five hundred students. When the school closed, a survey of the Boot Hill Graveyard uncovered thirty-one graves, though only twenty-four deaths were recorded. Ground radar then discovered more than fifty-five additional bodies.

The town of Marianna is still struggling through reports of the abuse from survivors, and the studies are proving many of the claims to be true. The extent of torture, abuse and claims of human trafficking may never be fully uncovered. As for now, the school grounds are off-limits until a new buyer can be found for the property.

Stories of hauntings flood the area around the school, and many of them center on the area that is now fenced in and far away from prying eyes. There is one area, though, that isn't fenced off and has many ghostly events associated with it. A church was built on the site to give the boys a proper Sunday service and a chance to find salvation. It was considered to be their one respite from the horrors of the school, and many survivors have said it was their only time of peace while kept there. Some said even there, abuse from other students would break out away from prying eyes, and rivalries would be finished in fights on the church grounds.

To this day, people say they see small shadows running around the old abandoned church. Paranormal hunters have recorded music and singing emanating from within the church's walls, though it has long been empty. Cries have also been heard echoing from the school across the road and are answered with what sounds like prayers coming from the church. Odd lights are seen through the old windows and the door at all hours—day or night.

The true horrors that occurred in Dozier have only recently been brought to light. During Hurricane Irma, some trees near the school were uprooted, and the crew that came to remove them detected more possibly unmarked graves. Another archaeological investigation began late in the summer of 2019. The Florida legislature issued a formal apology to survivors of the school in 2017. A memorial and reburial of the children has been proposed, but still no true solution exists. The town of Marianna is still fighting to clear itself of the reputation of Dozier, but it is intertwined with the school forever—a haunting legacy of its very own.

TALLAHASSEE

In 1821, shortly after Spain gave Florida to the United States, it was decided that a capitol needed to be built for the new territory. The two largest population centers were Pensacola and St. Augustine, and the Spanish had built a road between the two. It was decided that a point along that road—about halfway between the two cities—would be the most convenient place to build the capitol. The only problem was that some Creek Indians had a settlement right where they wanted to build.

At that time, Creek chief Neamathla ruled a city called Cohowofooche, which stood on the remains of an old settlement called Tallahassee. The previous settlement had been burned to the ground by General Andrew Jackson during the First Seminole War. Neamathla left grudgingly but came back a year later to fight for the land with six hundred warriors. He was rebuffed, and his tribe was forced to a reservation near Tampa. With a bloody past and a town founded on convenience, this location is brimming with quite a few ghost stories.

The most famous haunted location in the town is the grave of Elizabeth Budd Graham. It is often referred to as the "Grave of the Tallahassee Witch." There are many stories of her ghostly appearance at the grave site, and there are frequent sightings of black-robed figures attempting to summon her power from beyond the grave. Some claim she haunts their dreams, and her spirit follows them home.

In truth, this is very unlikely. Her marker is why so many ghost tours mention her. It is striking and stands out among the rest of the beautiful graveyard. The tall obelisk dwarfs all of the other stones. It faces west, which some say is contrary to Christian belief and is different from every other grave. This is not true, as several graves at this cemetery do face west, and many different denominations of Christianity insist on west-facing graves. Its orientation seems to be a matter of her location at the corner of the graveyard.

The second remarkable thing about her grave is a large inscription on the base of the marker, which some think is an eerie spell-like incantation. The truth is that it is simply a snippet from Edgar Allan Poe's famous work of poetry "Lenore." If you read the rest of the inscription, you'll realize that this was a woman adored by a wealthy husband, who built a showpiece for his tragically lost love.

This is not to say the graveyard is free of its fair share of supernatural sightings and unexplained events. Due to the grave of Elizabeth Graham, many paranormal research teams congregate here in hopes of finding or communicating with her spirit and getting the true story. Many local groups have recorded EVPs and documented shadowy figures among the graves during their frequent investigations.

Not far from her grave are the graves of Prince Charles Louis Napoleon Achilles Murat and his wife, Catherine Willis Gray. Murat was a nephew of Napoleon Bonaparte who came to Florida and owned a large piece of land near Tallahassee. The twin obelisks marking their graves are also quite remarkable to behold. Their spirits have also been seen near their grave site.

Another nearby infamous location is the Chi Omega sorority house at Florida State University. This is the house where Margaret Bowman and Lisa Levy were bludgeoned to death by serial killer Ted Bundy. The horrors of this tragedy include brutality on such a scale that it is difficult to explain them without sensationalizing the events.

The ghosts here are known to try to protect the students living in the house. Lights will often turn on in dark hallways, and a strange force once kept a young coed from opening her dorm room door. She later found out that her ex-boyfriend turned stalker had snuck into the building and was trying to find her. He was arrested after security guards spotted him climbing out of a window. She believes the ghost saved her life.

The Velda Mound Park is on the outskirts of Tallahassee. This mound dates back before the Seminoles or their Creek predecessors. It now belongs to the Fort Walton culture, which is a slight regional variation of the Mississippi culture of Native Americans. This mound is located in the Arbor Hill neighborhood in a housing estate and is tricky to find. It is now a state park and open to the public.

In the old city cemetery lies the imposing grave of Elizabeth Graham. *Courtesy of author.*

One day, a jogger called the fire department when he saw several people sitting by a large bonfire on the mound. He knew fires were not allowed in the area, and he feared it would spread. The fire department arrived at the site quickly, and firefighters even talked of seeing smoke as they drove up.

However, there was no blaze when they arrived. There was not even the sign of a blaze. The fire and figures had vanished.

One early morning, a young lady came to the Velda Mound Park to walk her small rescue dog. She lived nearby and had been there many times before. The sun had not yet come up, but she saw a strange glow from behind a nearby tree. Her dog began to whimper and tried to run away, but she held the leash tight. The glow grew brighter, and she stared in disbelief as a large, glowing white wolf came from behind the tree. She stated that the wolf looked like it had walked out of the tree. It was nearly twice the width of the tree and could not have been hiding behind it. The glowing wolf slowly walked up the mound and reared back to howl. It vanished just as the sun crested the hill. To this day, she claims she sees the large glowing beast in her dreams and wakes just before he begins to howl.

Other haunted locations in the city of Tallahassee include the Lively Building, which housed a notorious bar called the "Leon Bar" in the early 1900s. Here, ghostly cowboys are seen playing cards and walking around the old bar area. The Knott House Museum proudly displays pictures of ghosts that staff members have taken over the years. It also hosts frequent paranormal investigations for a modest donation to the museum.

THE BIG BEND

Apalachicola, Cedar Key and Tate's Hell

The area where the panhandle of Florida starts its turn south along the Gulf of Mexico is informally called the Big Bend. There are not any official markers for it, but most Floridians agree that it generally stretches from Apalachicola to Cedar Key. How far inland it goes is still a matter of debate. There is a small town called Big Bend, just north of Tampa, that would be the extreme southern edge of that wide expanse of the Sunshine State.

Apalachicola is a small beach town where the Apalachicola River meets the Gulf of Mexico. Its name comes from the Hitchoti Indian words *apalachi* and *okii*, thought to mean "the other side" and "people." The tribe that settled here was known as the Apalachicola people, or the "People on the Other Side of the River." The tribe here was estimated to have numbered nearly forty thousand people. They called this location home from around 2000 BCE until sometime in the mid-1400s. No one knows why they left the area, but only a small tribe remained when Panfildo de Narvaez landed with his conquistadors in the early 1500s.

The Spanish used the area as a port area in their early explorations. They used the river to explore farther inland. It stayed in Spanish hands until it was ceded to the British and then was given back to Spain before finally being given to the United States. The city was a boomtown of trade and one of the busiest ports along the Gulf of Mexico.

In 1837 Thomas and Sarah Orman moved to the area to expand their lucrative business dealings. Thomas had built one of the most beautiful homes in Apalachicola for his wife. It sits on a large hill overlooking the meeting of Scipio Creek and the Apalachicola River. The house has porches along the northeast and southeast sides of two stories, and intricate woodwork marks the front entrance. The Orman family owned the house until 1994, when it was sold to a couple that ran it as a bed-and-breakfast. It was eventually sold again—this time to the State of Florida. It is now the Orman House State Park and is open for daily tours.

Inside the house you will find many antiques from the early days of Florida and some original items of the Orman family. Many say the ghosts like to keep things neat and tidy, as though they still own the place. There are stories of visitors feeling slaps on their hands when they get too close to select artifacts in the home. Others have reported seeing strange shadows on the upper floors.

Behind the house, away from the wonderful view of the river, is a small covered well. Dug for the home, the stone pit goes deep into the bluff the Orman house sits on—down to the waters below. A legend says that a young girl was hiding from Union troops who had occupied the town during the Civil War, and she climbed into the well to avoid being harmed by the soldiers. She fell and died in the well, and her body was never recovered.

The haunted well behind the Orman House. *Courtesy of author.*

Her restless spirit has been seen floating out of the well, as though pulled upward by a strange glowing light, in late evenings. Her broken body walks with a strange gait because of her shattered bones. Her neck is twisted at such an odd angle that it is impossible to tell which way she is facing. She leaves damp, muddy prints as she walks toward any witnesses of this horrific vision. While there are no records of her death, and there are many who say the house is where most of the activity lies, many ghost hunters go to the well to see what they can find.

James N. Coombs came to the area just after the Civil War to establish several sawmills in Jackson County. Timber became one of the area's chief industries, and Coombs became one of the wealthiest businessmen in the area. He built a private home for him and his wife and hoped it would rival the beauty of the nearby Orman House. His wife truly loved the place.

Sadly, the grand home was ravaged by a fire in 1911, and the Coombs family had to relocate to a nearby hotel. Mrs. Coombs fell ill and died just a few days later. Could it have been the loss of her beloved home that did her in? Nobody is sure. But what we can be certain of is that her husband died

The Coombs Inn was severely damaged in a fire. Guests now frequently claim to wake sweating and feeling oppressive heat in the room—even on cold nights. *Courtesy of author.*

less than three weeks later. They are buried together at the Chestnut Street Cemetery, right across from their now-restored home.

The house is now a bed-and-breakfast called the Coombs Inn. Guests and staff say that you are almost guaranteed a ghostly experience if you stay in rooms five or eight. There are reports of poltergeist-like activity—objects being moved or thrown and simple knocking or tapping sounds on headboards while guests are trying to sleep. Most agree the spirits do not seem angry, but mostly playful. Could it be the Coombs family entertaining guests the only way they know how?

In 1907 the Franklin Inn was opened by L.G. "Jeff" Buck. He had seen the port of Apalachicola boom with the turpentine and lumber trade and knew it needed a nice hotel to help service the town. Being in the turpentine business, he saw to it that only the best trees were used in the hotel's construction. In 1914 he added a third floor to accommodate the influx of people wanting to stay at the first-class hotel.

His family sold the hotel a few years later to Annie Gibson Hays and Mary Ellen Gibson. The two ladies were successful entrepreneurs in their own right and had a famous hostelry nearby. They renamed the hotel the Gibson Inn and ran it until 1942, when the army took control of the building during World War II. It was used as a field hospital and garrison headquarters. The army gave it back to the Hays and Gibson families just after the war.

The hotel went downhill and was destined for the wrecking ball by the end of the 1970s. In 1983, however, the building was saved by an investment group that poured more than $1 million into restoring the hotel to its former glory. Almost immediately after reopening, the ghost stories began.

Someone—perhaps a guest or soldier—died of pneumonia in the house. His rasping cough is often heard along the third-floor hallway. Guests have woken in the middle of the night because they could hear the unseen spirit coughing in their rooms—perhaps in their own beds.

Other reported sightings of ghosts in the hotel include soldiers and even a young lady in an early-1930s style swimsuit, who waves as she runs out of the front door toward the park. A famous ghostly legend of twin girls being attacked by birds near the house seems to have been dreamed up by someone who watched too many movies. No solid reports or corroborating evidence support that story. But with so many other ghosts and plenty of witnesses, there is no need to make up stories at this inn.

A little north of Apalachicola, on the road to Sumatra, is a dark stretch of Highway 65. As travelers cross a set of railroad tracks, they should be on

The Gibson Inn was built in 1907 and is haunted by a ghostly sea captain and the infamous Grey Lady. *Courtesy of author.*

the lookout for an antique hearse that will pull up behind them. The old car will gain speed until it is dangerously close to the rear bumper. Its headlights will seem impossibly bright, intensifying the situation even further. Witnesses say they have been driven off the road or forced to pull over out of sheer terror as the hearse speeds on. Other witnesses who have experienced the hearse say that if you don't get out of its way, someone in your family will die that night. There have been so many reports of this car that a nearby road is called Bloody Bluff Road. The hearse never crosses that intersection, according to legend.

The area to the south and west is home to Tate's Hell State Forest. Cebe Tate's legend is one of Florida's strangest stories, and that's saying something. Cebe was the son of Jebidiah Tate and his wife, who was half Cherokee. Jebidiah was a Civil War veteran and had bought a huge amount of land in Florida for only five dollars, thanks to the Homestead Act. It was a tough place to work, but Jebidiah and his wife found a local Indian medicine man who offered to make them a deal. The man said that if Jebidiah gave him one pig a year, their farm would prosper, and the storm gods would stay far

One of the entrances to the aptly named Tate's Hell. *Courtesy of author.*

away. Cebe's mother knew the strength of Indian medicine and convinced her husband to take the deal. For years, the farm prospered, and they gave the medicine man his pick of the pigs every year.

When Jebidiah's wife passed away, it was too much for the old man. In anger, he refused to give the medicine man his pig that year. The old Indian warned him that if he broke the deal, not only would the land be broken but the family would go through hell. Jebidiah still refused to part with an animal. Jebidiah caught malaria shortly thereafter and died. Cebe tried to run the farm on his own, but the scrub cows died, the crops were stunted and even the trees seemed to dry up and stop producing oil for the turpentine plants. The only things doing well were his pigs. They ate and bred so fast that he had to build a second pen to contain them.

Cebe couldn't keep up with the farm, so he sent away for a mail-order bride from New York. He got a German immigrant, who was the ideal strong worker. The only problem was that she was Jewish and could not eat pork. After eating only potatoes and dried vegetables for a short while, she insisted Cebe go get her some meat.

In the spring of 1875, Cebe Tate and his hunting dogs went into the scrubland forest just off his family farm. He was not seen again for two weeks. He came out of the forest more than fourteen miles away in the town of Carrabelle. He had been bitten by numerous bugs and was delirious from a snake bite. The people of Carrabelle asked who he was and where he came from.

Malnourished and almost dead, he said, "My name is Cebe Tate and I've been through Hell."

Some say there are more ghosts than guests at the Island Hotel in Cedar Key. It is an amazing bed-and-breakfast either way. *Courtesy of author.*

The old Carrabelle Hotel survived a storm in the early 1900s. Guests often hear strange knocks on their door when storms come through the area. *Courtesy of author.*

The woods in this area are filled with stories of wild animals, giant swarms of mosquitoes and even some Skunk Ape sightings. The scariest parts of the area are the ghostly sightings of a lone, scared man screaming as he runs blindly through the brush, as though chased by the demons of Hell. Cebe Tate's spirit is still lost there today.

Carrabelle also has a notoriously haunted hotel. The Carrabelle Hotel was famously the last building standing when a hurricane struck the area. Everyone stayed inside the doors of the hotel, while the rest of the town was destroyed. The old hotel was remarkably unhurt. Visitors to the hotel speak of the sound of people knocking on their windows when storms pass through the area. Some say they can hear the pounding of hammers as though the doors and windows are being boarded up. One investigation group found dozens of thermal handprints pressing against the glass of one room when a sudden thunderstorm interrupted their investigation. Just be sure to sleep with one eye open in the Carrabelle Hotel.

AMELIA ISLAND

A melia Island is the northeasternmost point in Florida. The early Timucuan Indians inhabited the island and called it Napoyca until European explorers arrived and started fighting over the island. Early British settlers renamed the island after Princess Amelia, the daughter of Prince George II of Britain. The island has moved between so many empires that eight flags have flown over the island since its founding. It was once such a bastion of pirates and ne'er-do-wells that it even fended off a Spanish attack for a time. Today, the island includes the cities of Fernandina Beach, American Beach and Amelia City and, of course, is the home of many ghost stories.

The most famous ghost on the island is of the son of Louis-Michel Aury, Luc Simon Aury. Father and son were privateers and well-known pirates. Amelia Island has a deep seaport, even at low tide, which allows large ships into port at all times. This was crucial for smugglers and pirates to get their goods upriver and into the lands of the United States in the early nineteenth century. It is estimated that, at one point, more than four hundred ships were in the waters around the island, and nearly all of them flew the Jolly Roger pirate flag.

In 1817 a Scottish con man and mercenary named Gregor MacGregor, who was married to a cousin of revolutionary Simón Bolivar, sailed to Amelia Island with a force intent on seizing the land from the Spanish. MacGregor had swindled his way into power in South America and had built a small army after recruiting men from Europe to come to his fictional country of Poyais. In truth, it was simply the untamed jungles of Venezuela, and the fooled colonists all nearly died trying to help settle the area. MacGregor, however, gained control of Venezuelan armies and became a general in the Republican side of their revolution. He parlayed that control into even more power.

MacGregor came to Amelia Island with eighty men. The Spanish greatly overestimated his army and surrendered without firing a shot from their fort. He claimed the island as his own new kingdom, the Free Florida Republic. After holding it for a very short time, MacGregor tried to pay his own men with money he had printed, called Amelia dollars, and prohibited looting. Morale began to sink. He fled the island with his wife and headed back to Europe. When he arrived, he painted his experience in a good light, saying that he had been ordered to go by the Republic of Mexico and that he had sold the island to his good friend—the head of the Florida Republic Navy, Louis Aury.

Aury was a former French naval officer, who had become a privateer. He had made a name for his pirate crew by sacking a couple of undefended towns from Galveston to Mexico. Rival pirate Jean Lafitte had taken Aury's home base in Galveston while he was away sacking other towns. Aury received word about Amelia Island from his old friend Gregor MacGregor, and he set sail.

Aury sailed into port just two weeks after MacGregor had fled. He made some agreements with MacGregor's lieutenants who had been left in charge and took control of the island. He claimed the island for the Republic of Mexico and ruled the island starting in mid-September 1817. By the end of December that year, he had to surrender the island to U.S. troops who came to free the island and hold it "in trust" for Spain. They held it until 1821, when Florida was ceded to the United States.

Aury stayed for a couple of months after surrendering, supposedly to assist the transition. Instead, he helped smugglers and pirates continue to do their business. He made few friends among the local populace because none dared touch him out of fear of reprisals from the overwhelming pirate presence. When Louis Aury left the island, his son stayed behind because he enjoyed the sense of power. Without his father there to protect him, his crimes and societal offenses became too much for the locals to ignore. They arrested the young Aury, sentenced him to hanging and locked him in the town jail.

Young Aury realized he was being used as a tool of vengeance for the crimes of his untouchable father, not for his own misdeeds. He decided to deny the town the spectacle of his hanging and slit his own throat with a crude cutting tool he had carved from his bedding in the jail. A passing guard saw Aury bleeding out on the floor of his cell and quickly called the local surgeon. The surgeon saved Luc's life by stitching his throat back together. So that the town could have their hanging, the pirate's shirt was buttoned over the stitches for his walk to the hanging tree just outside the jail. He had no last words, but as the rope tightened at the moment of execution, it ripped the stitches and nearly removed the head of the notorious pirate. The blood spray covered the horrified crowd. Aury had gotten his revenge in a way he hadn't planned.

The old jail at Amelia Island still stands. It is the current home of the Amelia Island Historical Society and the Amelia Island History Museum. It holds an extensive collection of artifacts from Amelia Island's history, including many pirate artifacts. Luc Aury's spirit is also often seen here, with his head dangling from a small strip of flesh. The ghostly corpse wanders the halls dripping blood behind him. Many volunteers speak of having to clean unusual stains off the floor when they open in the morning.

The ghost of Luc Aury, who tried to slit his throat to escape justice at the end of a rope. Now he haunts the old jail with his head dangling to the side. *Illustration by Kari Schultz*.

At the northern point of the island lies Bosque Bello Cemetery. This haunted cemetery may be one of the most visually stunning cemeteries in Florida, which led the Spanish to name it "beautiful woods." The old trees and gravestones tell many tales from its centuries. It's no wonder there are many ghost stories here. Most famously, a voodoo queen's spirit is sought here to help find love and power. Her spirit is supposedly tied to several locations on the island, but her resting place hidden deep in old Bosque Bello Cemetery draws the most visitors.

During the pirate days of Amelia Island, the infamous pirate Blackbeard came to the port. His men came ashore and spent many days enjoying the comforts of the pirate havens on the island. One of Blackbeard's lieutenants split most of his time between the White House Brothel and a bar called Wicked Davey's. He fell in love with one of the women at the brothel, who told him the voodoo queen could help him kill Blackbeard and take his place as the true pirate king. With dreams of grandeur, he followed her to meet the queen.

The queen was named Mama Martina, and she told the lieutenant she could summon a loa spirit that would protect him from Blackbeard's sword. For a few gold coins and some blood offerings, he would be invulnerable to iron. He paid in full and went back to Blackbeard's ship to issue the challenge for command of the pirate fleet. As soon as he announced his challenge, Blackbeard thrust his sword to end the lieutenant's life. When he failed to hurt him, the young man smiled and drew his own blade to kill Blackbeard. Then Blackbeard drew his pistol and shot him. Perhaps he should have asked for protection from lead bullets as well.

When Blackbeard discovered the whole plot, he sought out the voodoo queen but failed to find her. He knew she had fled into Bosque Bello Cemetery and told his men to find her. When they all got lost in the twists of the cemetery, Blackbeard pulled his men out and fled the island, never to return. The queen's legend grew. Mama Martina is not a name commonly used for her, but it is the name of the only voodoo queen associated with the island that fits the period and the story. There are many unmarked graves in Bosque Bello—could hers be one of them? To this day, practitioners of the Hoodoo religion go to this cemetery to seek guidance from the spirit of Mama Martina.

Wicked Davey's was a notorious saloon on the island that dates back to the early 1800s. It housed several infamous murders and has long since closed. The building still stands and has had many tenants on its first floor. These former tenants claim to have heard noises in the unoccupied floors upstairs and have called the police at the sounds of arguments or gunfire. No one was ever found in any incident. Paranormal groups frequent this building for hunts as often as they can, due to the sheer volume of activity they can record on any given night.

The oldest saloon on Amelia Island is also the oldest continuously operating drinking establishment in Florida. The Palace Saloon is famously haunted by "Uncle Charlie," a bartender from the 1900s, who died in a room he rented upstairs in 1960. Charlie had invented a game in the bar where patrons would try to flip quarters into the cleavage of some of the carved wooden maidens above the bar. At the end of the night, he would collect all the failed attempts off the floor behind the bar and help himself to a nice profit. His spirit will often grab lost change behind the bar before anyone else can pick it up. Other spirits noted here include old patrons and a piano player who still plays the antique piano, though it is now encased in glass.

Other notable haunted sites on the island include the Eppes House, a historic home and private residence. Charlotte Eppes supposedly convinced her husband to kill a realtor in town who had made advances on her. The story claims were false, and she now haunts the house in payment for her crime. The Florida House Inn is one of the oldest hotels in Florida, and it contains the ghost of a sad man who gets into bed with lonely guests like himself. He is particularly wary of people who try to capture evidence of him.

Since our last visit to Amelia Island for *Eerie Florida*, the location of the legendary grave of Wiccademus has gone under development. The old trail has been bulldozed and housing plats are being constructed. By the end of 2019, people will be living on the site of one of Florida's most notorious urban legends. We are curious to see how this will affect the legend.

ST. AUGUSTINE

There are so many ghost books about St. Augustine, and so many ghost tours there, it is difficult to find a spot that is not haunted in the oldest city in the United States. The city is noted for being the first city established by the Spanish in their exploration of the land they called *La Florida*. Native Americans in the area inhabited the lands of St. Augustine for generations before that, though. No one is sure how long it has truly been inhabited.

The most iconic location in St. Augustine is the Castillo de San Marco. This old fort built by the Spanish is mostly made of coquina, which is a type of sedimentary rock that contains fragments of shellfish and other invertebrates, which turns into a sort of a natural concrete. The Spanish were very familiar with it from their homeland and found the supply in Florida suited their needs perfectly. The large fort has weathered storm after storm as well as pirate attacks, Civil War raids and fires. It still stands as a testament to Spanish engineering.

During the first period of Spanish control of the fort, the governor and commander had a young daughter who would travel with him to the fort quite often. She was very lovely, and the young soldiers were all quite enamored of her grace and beauty. The commander refused to allow any of the men to become too informal with his daughter because he was grooming her to marry someone at court in Spain. However, the young captain he placed to guard her had already captured her heart.

The two lovers kept the affair secret until the time came for her to be sent back to Spain to serve her purpose as a bride in an arranged marriage. She refused to leave and spoke of her love of the captain. The next day, the commander told his men that he was so moved by their love that he had them sent to Cuba to live on his plantation. The men were sad to hear of the loss of their captain but were happy for the young couple.

A few years later, some soldiers were moving the cannons on the battlements to new locations to prepare for a feared ground assault. The town had recently been burned by Sir Francis Drake with just such a tactic, and the new commander thought he could spare a few batteries from the seawall. When they moved the first cannon into its new home, it fell into the room below. The men went downstairs to find the cannon, but it was nowhere to be found. Men were called in to excavate a wall where they thought the cannon fell, and they found a hidden room that had been sealed up. A strong aroma of roses overwhelmed them. They found the cannon had crashed next to a couple of skeletons. The two had been lying in an embrace after being entombed in the secret room. They never would have been found if not for the falling cannon.

It did not take long for the men to deduce that this was the true fate of the young couple. The old commander's daughter was known to have always worn the scent of roses. The young captain's sword was also laying where he had attempted in vain to cut his way out of the room. The coquina hid their fate. Their ghosts now haunt the room, and you can still smell roses when their spirits are near. When touring the fort, the room is accessible through a crawl space into the large chamber.

A short distance away from the gates to the Old City, you will arrive at the old drugstore, which is now the home of Potter's Wax Museum. Built in 1789, but moved to its current location in 1887, the Old City Remedies building is a frequent stop on many tours, though its history is fairly inconsistent with the stories. However, it is true that Doctor Frederik Weedon helped care for the Native Americans incarcerated at the Castillo de San Marco, which was then called Fort Marion. The drugstore once famously housed the head of the old Seminole chieftain, Osceola, which Doc Weedon had removed from the body of the dead chief.

The old drugstore has many ghosts associated with it—most are old patients of the various doctors who lived there. Some say the spirit of Osceola goes there to look for his lost head. Most famously, though, many visitors feel a strong sense of vertigo or that they are being gassed at the drugstore. There have been reports of people passing out on ghost tours and paranormal investigations in the main lobby area, and some of these people have been hospitalized. No one can determine the source of this strange phenomenon, but there are theories of a mad doctor who gassed patients with chloroform before dragging them upstairs to do unspeakable acts.

If you continue down the road behind the drugstore, you will come upon Tolomato Cemetery. We discussed the large bust of Bishop Augustin Verot that stands tall above his grave in the center of the cemetery as well as his unusual funeral in *Eerie Florida*. As with all things in St. Augustine, though, there are even more stories to tell. No one is sure exactly how old the cemetery is because many of the graves are unmarked, but the Native Americans in the area used it as a burial site for possibly thousands of years before the founding of St. Augustine.

In 1821 Colonel Joseph Smith, a War of 1812 hero, moved to St. Augustine to be the territorial judge for the new state. Shortly after his arrival, he met a young couple that lived nearby, and they became fast friends. He would be the husband's mentor as he began to try his hand at law. Sadly, the young wife fell ill the next evening and was pronounced dead by the end of the week. The husband insisted that the colonel attend and help lead the funeral procession. The family placed the dead woman in a funeral chair instead of a casket, which was not uncommon at the time. As the procession passed under the Apopinax tree located next to the cemetery gates, the girl's head bumped a low-lying branch. Fresh blood appeared, and the colonel saw her blink. She was rushed to the colonel's home where she was miraculously revived a few days later. She had merely been in a coma, and she lived for another six years. At that point, she fell ill again and was once again paraded to the cemetery after being laid out for a week to make sure she was truly dead.

Her spirit is often seen wandering the graves of Tolomato in her white burial gown. She walks among the graves and stops to marvel at the statues and stones that have arrived since her death. She also often walks to the tree and stares blankly at it as though remembering when it hit her head. Was she buried alive again?

In 1877 tragedy struck Tolomato again. A young boy named James P. Morgan, who may have been named after the famous banker and business tycoon, lost his grip while playing in the old oak tree just inside the cemetery. He fell to his death and broke his neck. He was only five years old.

In 1972 a family moved into the house on the side of Tolomato, and their young son often played in the cemetery. He told his family about the young boy he played with in the cemetery named James. The family wanted to

No one is sure how many people are really buried at Tolomato Cemetery. *Courtesy of author.*

meet the boy and his family, but their son told them James said they could never meet him. When they asked around town, they discovered the story of the ghostly young boy in the cemetery and told their son he was never allowed to play in the cemetery again.

The ghosts of young James and the lady in white are seen so often at Tolomato Cemetery that it is a must-see stop on every ghost tour in town. The cemetery is closed after dark but is open to visitors on the third Saturday of each month from 11:00 a.m. until 3:00 p.m. When you go, say hi to all of the spirits.

Most famously, in the heart of town is Flagler College and what was once the princely Ponce de Leon Hotel, which was built by the famous oil baron Henry Morgan Flagler. Built entirely out of coquina and poured concrete, the hotel still dominates St. Augustine and is quite impressive. Henry Flagler made sure no two rooms in the Ponce were exactly alike, and he insisted that construction be as close to perfection as man could allow. One of the men laying tiles in the main hall famously told him that the room was perfect. Flagler bent down, moved a tile slightly and said, "Only God is perfect."

When he died, Flagler requested that all of the doors and windows remain open to allow his spirit to leave for heaven. A janitor, however, closed all of the doors and windows because he feared a coming storm. Suddenly a huge storm gale began to blow, and the janitor raced to close the rest of the doors. Supposedly, as the janitor shuttered the last window, the spirit of Henry

Flagler College and Ponce de Leon Hall dominate the center of St. Augustine. *Courtesy of author.*

Flagler slammed into a tile just below the closed window, where a picture of his face is still visible.

Flagler's spirit is by no means alone here. His second wife, Ida Flagler, is said to haunt the hotel. Supposedly driven mad by her husband's affairs, she spent some time committed to a sanitorium. She spent a considerable amount of time in the old hotel and was often found murmuring to the statues and paintings. Her spirit is still seen continuing this practice.

Flagler's mistresses were frequently quartered in an unusual room on the fourth floor. This large room is ornately decorated and nearly covered in mirrors. Researchers claim the room may have originally been designed to contact the dead and hoped it would keep his wife out of the room due to fear. When his wife found one of his mistresses in the room, though, she forced Henry to lock the mistress in there for days. This mistress apparently went mad and eventually hanged herself on one of the chandeliers in the room.

The space is now mostly used for storage but once housed students. It had to be closed due to all of the strange occurrences—from objects being thrown to strange screams heard in the night, no student would stay for long. The room is also known to be intensely cold—even on the hottest Florida summer night.

There are other ghosts considered to be past guests of the hotel, including a lady in a blue dress from the 1930s and a small boy who plays in the courtyard. There are legends about these ghosts, but most are pure speculation.

While in St. Augustine, you can eat at O.C. White's, which is one of the most haunted restaurants in the city. Once known as the Worth Mansion, the building was moved to its current location in 1960 after being in its original location since 1791. The building is haunted by several ghosts, including the former owner, Ms. Worth, whose husband was General Worth for whom Fort Worth Texas was named. Ms. Worth haunts the upstairs and is often heard arguing in the old office area, which is now behind a closed door.

Just a short distance from Tolomato lies the Prince of Wales Tavern, a British pub with a ghost story of its own. Fey Shelton owned the house where the tavern is now located. She worked at the pharmacy on St. George Street, and the story says that she was a mean-spirited lady who chased away anyone who came to visit.

She once reluctantly hired a man from the town to fix her stairwell railings, but she was unhappy with the job and chased the man out of her house. According to the legend, she fell from those stairs and wasn't found for several days. However, the truth is that Ms. Fey Shelton died in Flagler Hospital in 1983. There was no need to sensationalize her death, but it was the easiest explanation for the spirit in the building because hers is the only recorded death concerning the house.

The spirit here at the Prince of Wales Tavern is preceded by a rank odor, though only some seem to be able to notice it. It is often smelled at the top of the stairs before a shadowy shape forms out of the corners of the small area. Witnesses say the sense of unease in the building will grow just before the apparition manifests. An unseen force will then try to push witnesses down the stairs.

Note that while some witnesses swear this has happened to them, others in their group have been oblivious to the whole incident while standing right next to them. Is this another situation where the more susceptible you are to spiritual activity, the more likely you are to be attacked by a presence?

The pub downstairs is largely free of unusual activity, but the patrons often say they hear unusual sounds upstairs and see the shadowy form moving quickly at the top of the stairs. Since it houses some of the best fish and chips in the United States, it is a must visit. Just keep your eyes open

The St. Augustine Lighthouse has hosted so many ghostly investigations that it is often hard to find a night that is not booked months in advance. *Courtesy of author.*

while dining at the Prince of Wales.

Everyone who visits St. Augustine and looks for ghosts mentions the St. Augustine Lighthouse, which is known for its spectral keeper, who wanders up and down the stairs. The lighthouse keeper lost his two young daughters while they were playing on a rail line built to haul the stones to construct the house across the island. The little girls' spirits are often seen playing in the yard just outside of the house. The keeper is often seen in the lower floor of the home next to the lighthouse.

The old jail in St. Augustine houses so many ghosts that they could fill a book alone. A great tour goes into the old jail at night and has reenactors play these spirits as visitors walk through the old cells and to the mock gallows outside. Many folks on the tour have described watching the hanging reenactment on the gallows. However, while the tour guide talks about the gallows and the hangings, they never re-create them. So, what are the witnesses really seeing?

There are so many more ghost stories to tell about St. Augustine. While we'll continue our research, please don't hesitate to visit the Sheriff's Ghost Walk Tours if you want a lot of history and entertainment to go along with your St. Augustine ghost adventures. The Ghosts and Gravestones Tour will take you through the lighthouse grounds and into the old jail at night. Other tours take you through the oldest house, the St. Francis Inn and many more locations.

THE SPACE COAST

Daytona, Cocoa Beach and Rockledge

On the Atlantic side of Florida, there is a long stretch of beach along US 1—from Daytona Beach to just south of Cape Canaveral. The towns that populate this area cater to tourists and locals trying to get away from the crowded theme park areas. Due to its frequent visible launches into space from the Cape, the whole area came to be known as the Space Coast of Florida.

Daytona Beach sits at the north end of the Space Coast and is known for its tourist shops, such as the world-famous Ron Jon Surf Shop and, of course, the Daytona 500. What many don't know is that the town has several haunted locations worth a quick trip for those interested in looking for spirits while on spring break or watching the race.

The Clarendon Hotel on Atlantic Avenue in Daytona Beach opened in 1888. Unfortunately, it was destroyed by a fire in 1909. The hotel was then rebuilt and opened again as the Plaza Hotel in 1911, and the old hotel has always been known for stories of ghosts from the fire. These stories came to a head in 2013, when a security camera caught something unusual by the bar area of the hotel. Many claimed it was a spirit, while others claimed it was a bug on the lens. Either way, the hotel came back into prominence among paranormal aficionados and researchers.

A story resurfaced about a man who committed suicide in room 1111. He jumped to his death from the window in the mid-1970s. Many folks have claimed the door to the room will refuse to open, as though being held fast by someone inside. Then, suddenly it will spring wide open like someone let go of the other side. Other witnesses say there are strange noises in the hall outside the room all night. Guests often ask to transfer rooms because of the smell of smoke that permeates within.

Daytona Beach is famous for its yearly Bike Week, where motorcycle enthusiasts gather from all over to celebrate in the city. One of the longest-serving biker bars is a place called Boot Hill Saloon. This bar is home to the ghosts of old bikers who have died on the road to Bike Week. The spirits turn on the jukebox—even when it is unplugged. There are also sounds of pool games in the bar, though the pool table was removed some time ago. There have even been sightings of bikers in the bar as employees are locking up at night. One bartender claims it happens so often that he doesn't even bother to check if they are real anymore.

Just down US-1 lies the town of Rockledge, which is home to one of the most famous haunted restaurants in the world. A former train depot in town was converted into a bar called Jack's Tavern. In 1934, nineteen-year-old Ethel Allen was last seen alive here. Her body was discovered a few miles away on the banks of the Indian River. Her murderer was never caught,

The Wakulla Suites is now a Westgate Resort and home to a tragic suicide. *Courtesy of author.*

but many people suspected one of the employees at Jack's Tavern.

Jack's Tavern changed hands many times over the years and is now Ashley's Restaurant. The owners of the restaurant are quite proud of their resident ghost and display pictures from paranormal investigations on the walls. The story is on the back of the menu, and they allow groups to investigate overnight for a small fee. Most witnesses say Ethel's spirit is seen near the ladies' restroom on the first floor. A darker, more malevolent, presence on the second floor is known to try to force people back downstairs and even to try to break cameras and equipment by knocking it out of their hands.

A short distance away in Cocoa Beach, you will find what was once the Wakulla Suites Hotel. It is now a luxury Westgate Resort but was built in a tiki style in the 1960s. It was thought to be the safest place to stay on the beach during hurricane parties. After closing and becoming an apartment building until the early 1980s, it saw continual decline until being purchased and remodeled in its new form.

Always check your closets at the Wakulla Suites. *Illustration by Kari Schultz.*

Sometime during its brief tenure as the original hotel, something tragic occurred to one of its guests. A birthday clown, who had been a big hit while Bozo the Clown was on television, was realizing his career was coming to an end. Clowns had begun to lose their luster and appeal to the youth as television and movie spectacles became the new popular entertainment kids enjoyed. Down to his last dime, he had lucked out and gotten a gig at a local beach resort for one big shindig with the city of Cocoa Beach. Television crews were even going to be there, and it was a chance to start fresh.

When a storm hit, the event was cancelled. He was called and told he would not be compensated for his time. He decided to hang himself in the closet of the hotel room rather than go on. Or so the story goes. While we could find no records of any suicides in the hotel, the building's records are very spotty. During the 1970s, while it was an apartment complex, large groups were staying in the rooms, and police raided and arrested dozens of people on nearly a weekly basis. LSD, cocaine and other drugs were often seized at the complex. While there are no records of overdoses, there was a report of a bust of people dressed like clowns who were behaving indecently on an upper balcony facing the beach.

This story could be a combination of both of these urban tales, but there are witnesses who have seen a vision of a ghostly clown hanging in a closet in the old hotel. There are also reports of the sounds of crying and a suddenly strangled cry coming from a neighboring room. This story is so unusual that while many paranormal groups have tried to investigate it, they have yet to even identify which room the haunt is located with any accuracy.

Other nearby haunted places include the Georgianna Cemetery on lovely Merritt Island, which is home to many ghosts, including a small little girl who has been seen and photographed quite often. She is frequently seen sitting on various tombstones with the ghost of an elderly lady, as though telling each other stories. Some people claim that if you visit without paying proper respect, you will be pelted with stones from an unseen force that protects the cemetery from those wishing to cause harm to those at rest.

THE I-4 DEAD ZONE

Cassadaga and Sanford

Just between Daytona and Orlando lies a stretch of Interstate 4 that bisects Central Florida. This area is known as the I-4 Dead Zone. We discussed the story that gives the area its name in our previous book, *Freaky Florida*, but as is always the case in Florida, there are so many more stories to tell about this stretch of land.

The most spiritually famous town in this area is Cassadaga—a spiritualist commune that was founded by a psychic who had been led here by his spirit guide in the 1930s. He built a grand hotel overlooking the two hills, and to this day, the Cassadaga Spiritualist Camp hosts psychics, mediums and spiritualists from all over the world.

For many years, the town tried to hide the ghostly presences in the area. They tried to focus on what the camp believed were the positive sides of spiritualism. They even went so far as to make sure there was no mention of the Cassadaga Cemetery anywhere in the city because it was actually just beyond the city limit—in the neighboring community of Lake Mary. It was as though the town was hiding the ghosts.

Now things are much different. There is a weekly ghost tour in the hotel, and spirit mediums are as prevalent in the community as the tarot readers of old. The bookstore and gift shop now sell paranormal books along with spiritual self-help books. The town also has a new motto: "Where Mayberry Meets the Twilight Zone."

Ghosts at the hotel include George Colby, the founder of the hotel, who wanders around checking on his guests. Another famous ghost is Arthur—

The beautiful Cassadaga Hotel is home to psychics, clairvoyants, spiritualists and mediums. *Courtesy of author.*

an Irish guest from the 1930s who loved cigars and whiskey. He was a tall, thin man and loved the old hotel. His spirit is often seen walking the upstairs balcony and hallways. He tends to be drawn out by those smoking on the veranda.

We debunked the infamous Devil's Chair of the Cassadaga Cemetery in *Eerie Florida*, but it does not mean the cemetery is not haunted. Many paranormal teams have investigated the cemetery and even made contact with some of the spirits in the cemetery via EVP and other means. One session recorded talking to the Thatcher family, whose plot houses Devil's Chair. According to the recordings, they started the legend of Devil's Chair to keep away kids and vandals but did not realize it would have the opposite effect.

Farther east, across Lake Mary, lies the town of Sanford. Sanford was once the celery capital of the world and even has a main road called Celery Avenue, though the farms are long gone. There is, however, a ghostly horse that still races alongside cars on the road. There is a legend of an old hostler who had a shop on the road. He had a horse so large that when it died, a tractor had to drag it to the grave site. Many people believe this is the spirit horse seen along the road. Others say the horse is ridden by a Native American spirit. The area was once burial lands for the natives of the area, so this may be the real reason for the apparition.

ORLANDO

If we were to realign the United States based on most popular destinations, our nation's new capital would be Orlando, Florida. With all of the theme parks and neighboring tourist attractions, it is one of the most popular destination for visitors from all over the world, but it wasn't always this way. The area only bloomed after the founding of Walt Disney World in 1971.

These tourists almost never see what natives refer to as "The Real Orlando." Walt Disney World and Universal Studios are some distance away from the city proper. More's the pity. They are missing one of the most unique cities in Florida.

The area was once called Fort Gatlin after Doctor John S. Gatlin, who had been killed in the Dade Massacre during the Second Seminole War. The change of the name to Orlando is quite a legend itself. Was it named after the Shakespearian character from *As You like It* or a lost grave of a murdered traveler? There are several guesses, but the most popular version is that an early politician named Judge Speer named the town after the character, but he used the legend of a murdered farmer named Mr. Orlando, who got sick and died as he passed the town. They would often use his grave as a travel marker.

Where the grave lies, let alone if there even is a grave, is often contested. Many people believe it is one of the many graves at Greenwood Cemetery near the heart of downtown Orlando. Founded in the 1880s, after a famous newspaper campaign to make a proper city cemetery, Greenwood opened its gates and is still in use today. It now covers more than eighty-six acres of land with a thirteen-acre park next to it.

There are so many graves here that an accurate account is difficult to find. A large number of the graves belong to children because Sunland, an infamous children's hospital, was close by. The areas where the children are interred are referred to by the caretakers as "Baby Lands." They are numbered for navigation in the sprawling cemetery.

Sunland Hospital was originally built as a tuberculosis hospital but was converted to the poorly named Sunland Training Center for Retarded Children. This hospital remained in operation for many years, and there were many allegations of neglect and abuse. Many of these claims were backed up by witness accounts and health code violations. The hospital was finally closed and sat abandoned for a number of years before being demolished in 1999.

People often hear the laughter and cries of children as they visit the Baby Land areas. Many visitors claim to feel tugs on their clothes or even ghostly hugs on their legs as though from a small child. Paranormal investigators frequent these areas due to the large amount of spectral activity. Many go to the park where Sunland once stood and visit both locations to try to make contact with ghostly children.

Veterans from both sides of the Civil War, the Spanish-American War, both world wars and more are buried in special areas of Greenwood as well. There is also a large number of unmarked graves in one portion of Greenwood. This area is the home of many African American lynching victims. One of these victims was July Perry, who was hanged in 1920 and was finally given a gravestone in 2002. He had been attacked because he tried to vote in the election that year.

The ghosts and stories of this graveyard could fill this entire book. The most famous ghost here is a mysterious lady in white with a dark face and glowing, red eyes. She is often seen through a ray of moonlight as she walks past the grave markers in Baby Land Three. The mausoleum of Fred Weeks has a frequent spectral visitor near the top of the hill it sits upon. This shadow-covered figure is thought to be Fred Weeks himself, who often came to the graveyard and picked his plot personally.

A short drive downtown takes one to the Orlando Train Station. This area was once the home of Church Street Station. It was built by Bob Snow and designed after his successful Seville Quarter in Pensacola. Now it is the home of Central Florida's SunRail trains and is a popular nightlife and dining destination.

A restaurant here, called Hamburger Mary's, serves gourmet burgers and an excellent array of drinks. It was a hardware store at one point and is

Cevíche in Church Street Station in downtown Orlando has a haunted mirror behind the bar and many ghosts in the building. *Courtesy of author.*

the home of two well-known ghosts. A lady in an early-1900s dress is often seen wandering around the place. Many patrons thought she was a hired character, as is common at the nearby theme parks. The other ghost is a little girl who knocks on the windows and walls as if trying to get the attention of her parents, who are long gone. There doesn't seem to be much history to back either of these ghostly presences, but there are so many eyewitness reports that it would be hard to dismiss them.

Across the street is the popular Spanish restaurant Cevíche. This bar is home to another ghostly lady in late Victorian attire, who is often seen staring into the long mirror behind the bar. Many people often stare into the striking mirror and claim to see people from other time periods sitting at tables in the mirror. When they turn around, the tables are either empty or occupied by other customers. The employees say they try not to look into the mirror. One bartender says he still has nightmares from seeing a strange man in a cowboy hat locking eyes with him in the mirror.

Nearby, Lake Eola is noted for having a ghostly dog that likes to play with people who walk their own dogs at the park. Another body of water, Lake Lucerne, is said to have a ghostly lady in a white gown who seems to be descending a stairway on an unseen boat over the water on moonlit nights.

NORTH CENTRAL

Clermont, Umatilla, Mount Dora and Ocala

A way from the tourist mecca of Orlando and far from the beaches of the coasts," is the best way to describe Central Florida. When you look at a picture from space of Florida at night, you'll see the brightly lit cities, but you'll also see large dark spots in the center of the state that are peppered with small areas of bright towns. The dark lands are mostly the Ocala National Forest and the Green Swamp. The towns on the outskirts of these two stretches of natural Florida are populated with those who want the Florida weather but don't want the hassle of the big cities.

The town of Clermont is a short drive off I-4 on US 27. The town was made infamous by a strange murder that occurred there and was featured on the *Unsolved Mysteries* television show. The show featured the murder of a man who lived at what is known as the Harden House.

The story involved a lady who kept dreaming about a house and running down the stairs. When she moved to Florida, she saw the house from her dreams in Clermont. The family purchased and moved into the home. Immediately, the family began to see and hear unusual things in the house—mostly noises and objects moving. One night they awoke to the sound of a music box. When they went downstairs, all of the music boxes in the owner's collection were open and playing at once.

She learned of the terrible unsolved murder that had occurred in the house and thought the ghost was trying to tell her how he died. The ghost appeared to her and her husband saw an apparition of the murderer. The episode ended with the case still unsolved, but reports of the ghostly activity

The Harden House was really the Hardin House and the basis for an infamous case on *Unsolved Mysteries. Courtesy of author.*

began to dwindle. It was noted that the crew witnessed some unusual activity while filming the episode.

The real murder that occurred there was of John Hardin, not Harden. He lived in the old Victorian house with his young daughter and his second wife, who had inherited the place in the mid-1970s. In 1975 John, who owned a refrigeration business, received a late-night call from a client. He took his whole family on the call. While they were out, the phone lines to the house were cut. After arriving home just before midnight, John took a shower.

When he left the shower, he saw out of the window that his truck was on fire. He quickly threw on some pants and a flannel shirt. His wife said she heard an explosion as she waited inside. Firefighters eventually arrived after a neighbor called in the fire. There was no explosion. John had been shot in the chest with a shotgun and was lying beside the burning truck. His murder has yet to be solved.

John Hardin was buried nearby at Monteverde Cemetery, and his grave was a military-issued marker. On the marker, his name is misspelled and his birth year is wrong. That may be why the house is called Harden House instead of Hardin House. John's ghost has frequently been seen on the street and coming down the stairs near the front door—still wearing the flannel shirt he was murdered in.

Not far away is the small town of Umatilla. In this town, there was a restaurant called Stanna's. With small apartments on the upper floors, the building has been occupied in one way or another for years. Stanna's was often considered to be a very haunted location that was home to a mysterious, dark figure with no fingers that would reach out for you. The large hulking shadow always was accompanied by a strange smell. When Stanna's went out of business, it was purchased and reopened as a Beef 'O' Brady's in the mid-1990s. During this period, a small ghostly boy began to be seen in the hallway toward the restrooms. The boy would laugh and play with customers and staff. He would seem to try to flee when the dark hulking ghost would arrive. Beef 'O' Brady's closed as well in just a few years.

Today, Gator's of Umatilla occupies the location. Staff and customers still see the large ghost with no fingers and the little boy who flees from him. One bartender spoke of a strange mist in the shape of a woman who has recently started appearing late at night to try to stand between the two other ghosts—as if to keep them apart. There are no records of anything that remotely fits the descriptions here, but the stories are compelling.

The town of Mount Dora is well known for being uniquely old Florida. Thanks to US 441 bypassing the city, it was able to stay off the beaten path and keep its historic charm. One of the oldest buildings here is what was once called the Alexander House. This home was actually an early Florida hotel. It was renamed the Lake House in 1893 because it sits on the shore of Lake Dora. The old Victorian-style hotel was renamed once again in 1903 and is now called the Lakeside Inn.

The Lakeside Inn is the oldest continuously operating hotel in Florida. It housed former presidents as well as Thomas Edison and Henry Ford before it became neglected over the years. It was privately purchased in 2011 and has undergone extensive renovations. The old hotel is quite stunning, and the serene landscape harkens back to old Florida as much as Ocala does.

The hotel has several ghostly inhabitants. The most infamous is the ghost of a fisherman who walks along the shoreline near the pool area. He is often seen gazing and pointing at the swimmers. When someone goes to chase him away, he simply vanishes. The strong smell of dead fish is often smelled when he is near.

There are ghost tours of the hotel nearly nightly and many opportunities to book the haunted rooms. A local paranormal investigation team hosts events at the hotel quite often if you are looking to visit with an experienced and equipped team of ghost hunters.

The Seven Sisters Inn across town is also said to be haunted. Some of the stories are echoes of those at the Lakeside Inn, so it is difficult to tell which might be supported by historical records. Employees we spoke with at the

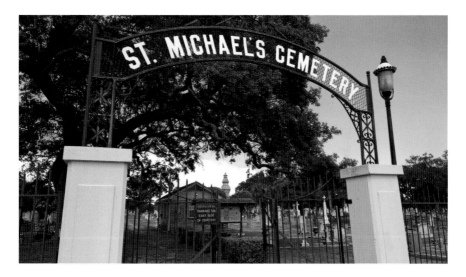

A large, glowing skeletal figure chased several navy sailors from St. Michael's Cemetery's late one evening in the mid-1940s. When it grabbed one of the sailors, he blistered at the touch. Keep a wary eye out after dark when visiting this cemetery—Florida's second oldest. *Courtesy of author.*

In Pensacola's Victorian Bed and Breakfast, guests often hear strange noises near the kitchen at night. They are awakened by the smell of cooking bacon, but the staff hasn't even started the stove. *Courtesy of author.*

The Seville Quarter was a refurbished factory, which was turned into a ragtime and jazz saloon. The original Rosie O'Grady's Goodtime Emporium is haunted by the ghost of a former bartender who died of hypothermia after falling in the walk-in freezer. Many poltergeist incidents at the location have been blamed on Wesley, the spectral barman. Other ghosts are thought to haunt the building as well. *Courtesy of author.*

The Brooks Bridge spans from Fort Walton Beach to Okaloosa Island and has a pack of spectral wolves that runs along the shore, then out toward the middle of the bridge over the waters below. They have a faithful schedule they like to keep. *Courtesy of author.*

Left: The Bellamy Bridge has a ghost story so famous that it is on the state park information sign at the start of the trail. Sadly, the legend doesn't match the history, but a ghost is still frequently spotted. *Courtesy of author.*

Below: The old jail on Amelia Island currently houses the Amelia Island History Museum and, apparently, one disturbed ghostly pirate. *Courtesy of author.*

There are many reports of ghostly apparitions among the gravestones. Some people even see ghostly children playing in the ancient trees that grow among the buried dead. *Courtesy of author.*

The Castillo de San Marco is one of Florida's most iconic landmarks and the oldest masonry fort in the United States. It is also home to a ghostly couple, whose bodies were found years after their disappearance when a cannon fell through the ceiling of their sealed and secret room. *Courtesy of author.*

The old jail has rebuilt gallows behind it. During ghost tours at night, tourists sometimes tell of reenactors showing their hanging. The tour guides, however, say that though they dress the part and tell the stories, no one reenacts the hanging. So, what are the visitors witnessing? *Courtesy of author.*

The Prince of Wales pub in St. Augustine is just down the street from Tolomato Cemetery and has a great ghost story of its own. A woman who owned the house fell to her death from the top of the stairs. Her ghost is seen in the windows outside or at the top of the stairs quite frequently. *Courtesy of author.*

Ashley's Restaurant in Rockledge has many photos on its walls of the spirits captured on camera here. If you capture something extra in your own photographs, they will happily add it to their ever-growing collection of spirits on film. *Courtesy of author.*

The sprawling Greenwood Cemetery could fill several books with amazing photos. Some areas are named like this one, which is filled with the graves of children from the nearby infamous Sunland Hospital. They call this area Baby Land 3. *Courtesy of author.*

Above: Boston Cemetery is near the University of Central Florida, and many students live in the apartment complex that surrounds this old cemetery. Most students avoid the graveyard because a hanging figure has been seen from one of the trees. Ghostly laughter echoes from the graves, as though children are playing among the tombstones. *Courtesy of author.*

Left: Sulphur Springs Tower is an iconic landmark of Tampa. No one knows how many have leaped to their deaths from its heights over the years. A great many did so during the Great Depression. The ghosts witnessed here are seen jumping to their deaths over and over again. *Courtesy of author.*

The infamous May Stringer House in Brooksville houses many ghosts. It was once the home of a doctor and a final resting place for many of his patients, whose graves nestle just beside the house. The scariest ghost in the house is known only as Mr. Nasty. He stays in the attic and earns his namesake by frequently attacking those who try to antagonize him. *Courtesy of author.*

The Vinoy Hotel sat abandoned for many years. It has been restored but contains many ghost stories. Visiting baseball teams have refused to stay at the hotel at all, but especially the third floor after many of them claimed to have been disturbed by the spirits there. The fifth floor has several ghosts as well, as documented on *The Ghost Hunters* television series. *Courtesy of author.*

Comfort Station Number One has several urban legends about its construction, but the ghosts here don't care about those at all. The spirits are heard scratching, knocking and even starting conversations with patrons while they are attending to the call of nature. Many psychics tell of a strong negative energy around the building. *Courtesy of author.*

The Don CeSar Hotel is one of the most iconic locations in all of Tampa Bay. A beautiful hotel with a tragic love story behind it, many ghosts have been reported here, including the creator of the hotel and many spirits from when it was used by the army as a hospital during World War II. *Courtesy of author.*

The Ca' d'Zan looks over Sarasota Bay on the grounds of the Ringling Museum of Art. The ghosts of John Ringling and his wife are often witnessed walking here or on the veranda. *Courtesy of author.*

The Flagler Mansion, also known as Whitehall, is in Palm Beach. It was the home of Henry Flagler and his wife. They both died within its halls, and their spirits walk the halls of the palatial mansion. *Courtesy of author.*

Left: The Colony Hotel's iconic elevator is host to many reports of ghostly activity. It is still run by the staff. *Courtesy of author.*

Below: The Boca Raton Resort and Spa is home to a pesky poltergeist. No direct stories name the ghost here. There are many accounts from guests and staff members of objects moving on their own throughout the resort. Items go missing from rooms, only to be found hours later in unusual locations. *Courtesy of author.*

Above: The Stranahan House in Fort Lauderdale is considered to be one of the most haunted buildings in Florida. At least six members of the Stranahan family have died in the house. Frank Stranahan killed himself by tying himself to the iron gate of the fence before jumping into the river behind his home. *Courtesy of author.*

Right: The infamous Riddle House is in Yesteryear Village. The ghosts are so active that they have been documented by several television shows, including *Ghost Adventures* on the Travel Channel. *Courtesy of author.*

The ValuJet Flight 592 memorial stands at the edge of the Everglades—a few miles south of the crash location just off US 41. It does double duty as the marker for the Eastern Airlines Flight 401 crash, which was just a few hundred yards away from the 592 site and has no marker of its own. *Courtesy of author.*

Ted Smallwood built his store on the banks of the Everglades. It was here that notorious criminal Edgar Watson was gunned down by the entire community in an act of vigilante justice. There were so many bodies found in the swamplands near the store, it's no wonder it is haunted. *Courtesy of author.*

The Blue Anchor Pub's façade and front door were more at home in Whitechapel, where it was built, than in Delray Beach, where it was moved. Two Jack the Ripper victims were known to have had their last meals through these doors when it was still in London. Could the Ripper have walked through them as well? *Courtesy of author.*

Gangster Fatty Walsh was killed on the thirteenth floor of the Biltmore Hotel in Coral Gables. His spirit still haunts the hotel. *Courtesy of author.*

The walls of Fort Zachary Taylor provided an excellent defense. Now they keep in the lost spirits, including a still-patrolling ghostly solider. *Courtesy of author.*

The Artist's House was the longtime home of Robert the Haunted Doll. Robert is now kept at the Fort East Martello Museum. He was locked in the tower of this house for decades. Guests say there are other ghosts that may have been here long before Robert and are still here now. *Courtesy of author.*

Captain Tony's Saloon was originally Sloppy Joe's Tavern. It was frequented by famed writer Ernest Hemingway. It has two graves inside, and an old hanging tree still grows up through the bar. *Courtesy of author.*

Marrera's Guest Mansion is home to the ghost of an evicted wife and her children. Enriquetta Marrera had no idea her husband's first wife even existed, but she came and took the house upon his death. Enriquetta and her children may never have truly left, for their ghosts are often heard in the upstairs rooms. *Courtesy of author.*

Seven Sisters Inn told tales of unusual noises and dark shapes, but they were nothing like the activity at the other hotel.

Pat Frank lived nearby in Tangerine, Florida. He wrote a post-apocalyptic novel, *Alas, Babylon*, and seemed to base his fictional town on Ocala. Shortly after its publication, several family members in town began construction on a secret bunker to survive an apocalypse like the one in Pat Frank's book.

If you ask some of the older families in Ocala, you might find someone who will admit that the Catacombs exist, but no one will tell you exactly where it is. Many natives claim the whole place is merely an urban legend. But it most certainly is not. The Catacombs was built. It still stands in an undisclosed location hidden behind some of the quaint shops. It is also very haunted.

A scandalous murder occurred there in the 1960s. According to the story, the murder involved a previous mayor and his son, both of whom had extramarital affairs with the daughter of a local judge, who was married to a prominent local attorney. The Catacombs was their secret meeting place until the girl was murdered. The crime was blamed on a local transient, though many people suspected one of the prominent townsfolk involved in the scandal was using the suspect as a scapegoat. When the man was lynched after being bailed out by a mysterious benefactor, the trial and case were simply hushed up. Her ghost can be heard wailing as she walks the halls of the empty catacombs.

St. Luke's Cemetery is home to this old turpentine shed, which was turned into its early chapel. Many visitors speak of a sense of unease and not being alone here. *Courtesy of author.*

Another ghostly location nearby is St. Luke's Cemetery. The original chapel in Oviedo is an old turpentine shed, and the small green building is the home of a dark entity who many people claim is the ghost of a vagrant child molester. The building does give off a sense of unease, but we could find no historical evidence to back up the legend.

BROOKSVILLE

The third-largest state forest in Florida is the Withlacoochee Forest. It has many trails, parks and plenty of old Florida forest to keep any nature enthusiast enthralled. The most popular area here is Silver Lake, with smooth grasslands near the lake and an amazing canoe trail and boardwalk. On the other end of the forest lies a darker place.

The Hog Island Trail near Brooksville lies on the east bank of the Withlacoochee River. It includes a two-mile loop trail and a deeper seven-mile trail into the forest. The campground has plenty of facilities for those staying overnight, but campers are also given a friendly warning: "Beware of the Hog Island Witch."

The legend goes that a witch lived in this area and helped locals in Brooksville with folk remedies and even some midwife services. When the harsh winters of 1894 and 1895 came around, the townsfolk blamed those who sought help from the witch in the swampy lands at the edge of the forest. They went out to find her and bring an end to her ungodly ways.

She was dragged to an ancient oak tree, and the whole town sat by through her screams while she was being put to death. There are diverging stories as to whether she was burned or hanged at the tree. A third version of the tale suggests she was hanged but would not die. After several agonizing hours, the leader of the group lit her on fire, and she burned while hanging. Whichever story is true, it was a horrible fate for the poor witch, who had helped so many in the town during times of need. But this was where she laid a curse on the town.

Locals refer to her as Swamp Water Maggie, but that may be because her story resembles the song "Swamp Witch" by Jim Stafford. The song is about Black Water Hattie, who lives near Lake Okeechobee on the opposite side of the state. Jim Stafford admitted he created the song from an idea he had with no basis on local legends, as we detailed in *Freaky Florida*. There are also no records to indicate that the legend is true. Today, though, campers often hear a woman's wailing and screaming echoing from the woods at night. Campers in tents have reported hearing the woman run her claw-like fingers along the side of their tent, and some witnesses have seen her burning body run past their campsite, while she screams into the night. Rangers and police are often called to the woods to investigate, but there are many reports that it was just someone pranking the campers by pretending to be the Hog Island Witch.

The Hog Island Witch story is well known in the area. One of the directors of *The Blair Witch Project*, which was written and produced by a group of friends in Orlando, claims that the legend was one of the chief inspirations for the film.

A recent episode of *Tripping on Legends*, a podcast by Christopher Balzano, included an investigation on Hog Island, where they wandered off the main loop trail. They found an old oak tree with an old noose hanging from a branch. *We* went out a week later and could not find the same rope, but it felt odd to be looking for the death site of a witch who still haunts the area.

Another haunted location in town is the Brooksville Train Depot. This train station was built in 1885 and is located in the historical heart of Brooksville. The line was once part of the great Plant System and ran track through Brooksville from nearby Croom and Centralia. The Hernando Heritage Museum Association acquired the building in 1991 and turned it into a train history museum. The station contains an amazing collection of artifacts from the early days of Brooksville and even has artifacts from Centralia, which is now a ghost town. It also houses some of the most notoriously active spirits, which draws paranormal investigators from all over the world.

Teams have learned of several spirits here, including "The Whistler," which creates a spectral tune that lasts for hours on end. Recordings of his eerie whistling can be heard on many YouTube videos taken during investigations. A strong odor precedes the appearance of one ghost known as "The Passenger." He tends to linger in the old train car just beside the station. For a $100 donation to the Hernando Historical Society, you can be locked into the depot with its many spirits for an evening.

The ghostly witch of Hog Island terrifies campers at the site of her hanging and burning. *Illustration by Kari Schultz.*

Across town lies what many consider one of the most haunted locations in Florida. In 1842 the Armed Occupation Act was enacted by the U.S. government. It stated that any settler who moved to Florida, lived on the land for five years and cultivated at least 5 acres with a dwelling would be granted 160 acres. Richard Wiggins took that offer and went to the area of Brooksville.

Wiggins sold a parcel of his land to John May in 1855. May built a four-room house on the land, and he lived there with his wife until he passed

The Brooksville Train Depot is a favorite spot for paranormal investigators from all over the world due to frequent ghostly activity. *Courtesy of author.*

away in 1858. May's wife, Marena, stayed in the house and continued to run the plantation they had created. She married Frank Saxon, a Confederate soldier, in 1866, and just a few years later, in 1869, Marena died during childbirth.

Saxon remarried and sold the house to Dr. Sheldon Stringer. Stringer began to expand on to the house, and it eventually had fourteen rooms and four stories. In some of the rooms the ceilings are ten feet tall. Dr. Stringer began to practice medicine in one of the rooms, and many believe he used some of the extra rooms to house patients. Three generations of the Stringer family lived in the house until selling it to Dr. Earl Hensley.

The Hensley family did not stay long and sold the house to the Hernando County Historical Museum Association in 1981. There are now exhibit rooms with various themes throughout the house. Each room tells a story of a different era—from the early pioneer days to military history and even an old doctor's office, which was built to resemble Dr. Stringer's practice.

The home also houses at least thirteen spirits, according to investigators. The most common spirit is that of Jessie May Saxon, the three-year-old daughter of Marena and Frank, who died in the home. She likes to play games with visitors and warns people to stay away from the attic where Mr. Nasty lives.

Not much is known about Mr. Nasty, but it is surmised that he was one of Dr. Stringer's patients. He is usually described as a dark, negative presence on the upper floors. He seems to enjoy tormenting visitors who seem susceptible to his presence. He is a violent spirit and does not take kindly to those who try to antagonize the spirits of the house. More pacifistic investigators, like Momento Mori Paranormal, disagree and say Mr. Nasty is actually nice to those who don't attempt to antagonize him.

Marena and Frank's spirits have often been seen in the house, as have many others. Tons of photographs and video evidence have been recorded in the house. The Hernando County Historical Society uses the money raised from hosting investigations to try to restore some of the damage from termites and Florida's terrible storms.

Driving farther into the outskirts of Brooksville, you can stumble across Spring Hill Cemetery. This is an old African American cemetery, where the ghost of a hanged man is said to be seen swinging from the large cypress tree in the middle of the graves. Shiloh Cemetery is not far away. This cemetery is home to several ghosts, including a Civil War soldier and a Native American who seems to transform into a spectral boar. These are just some of the many ghosts of Brooksville.

TAMPA

Tampa is known as the lightning capital of the world and, of course, as Cigar City. Originally, the Seminole tribe claimed this area after the Tocobaga Indians vanished. As the United States took possession of the area from Spain, they founded Fort Brooke at the mouth of the Hilsborough River and Tampa Bay. With a small population of civilians gathered near the fort, it was incorporated in 1855. The town floundered for years during the constant wars with the Seminole tribe and consistent outbreaks of yellow fever. It was unincorporated during most of the 1870s.

When Henry B. Plant brought his railroad to the area in the 1880s, it created a boom for the fledgling cigar, turpentine and phosphate industries. With an influx of Spanish, Italian and Cuban immigrants, the cigar capital was created in the Tampa neighborhood known as Ybor City. Tampa had jumped from eight hundred residents in 1880 to more than fifteen thousand in 1900.

Ybor City was founded in 1885 by several cigar manufacturers, including Don Vicente Martinez-Ybor. It mostly housed immigrants working in the cigar factories in the area. Each ethnic group founded its own mutual aid societies and labor organizations. Most of these groups built grand halls to show off their artisans and give the groups a meeting place. The Italian and German Clubs were each founded to help members from their respective communities, like the Cuban Club mentioned in *Freaky Florida*.

Ybor City made a deal with the City of Tampa that it would police itself and would handle any incidents and crimes within the borders of the neighborhood. Police would only be allowed in the community when needed or requested. This led to spotty record-keeping and many undocumented deaths and crimes. The City of Tampa, though, never pursued the matter, as it seemed to be easier to avoid the area. Everything seemed to be under control in the early days of the booming neighborhood.

During the Great Depression, demand for cigars diminished, and many of these immigrants had no other work available. Widespread unemployment and hardship swept the neighborhood, and it became a haven for smugglers and organized crime. Some historians believed a network of tunnels was built under the city at this time to assist in these illicit trades. Modern theories suggest the tunnels were actually part of an early sewer system that predated this era. The tunnels were simply enhanced by smugglers during Prohibition.

An infamous bordello opened just down the street from the Cuban Club on the upper floors of what was the American Cigar company headquarters. It was known for hosting a beauty pageant, which was judged by the mayor of Tampa and noted local officials. Winners would be allowed to work in the bordello. Since the area was still policing itself, such actions were never questioned.

Across the street was the Gonzales Clinic. Among the staff at the struggling hospital was one Doctor Avellanal. This gifted surgeon helped stop the worst of one outbreak of yellow fever among the dock workers. He didn't charge much for the burgeoning Spanish and Cuban population. He did, however, have one drawback—his son.

Avellanal Jr. wanted to be a doctor, just like his father. He studied hard but could never match his father. He also apparently suffered from schizophrenia and antisocial personality disorder. His father used his influence to house him at the bordello across the street, which was now very reputable and rumored to have housed Franklin Roosevelt and Winston Churchill on their visits to Tampa Bay. The young man used his father's credentials to get some of the girls to come up to his room so that he could treat them for their various diseases and infirmities.

Once he got them inside, he would perform experimental surgery and try sadistic methods to treat the young women. When they would finally expire, he knew he had to dispose of them. He took them down into the cellar and through one of the tunnels under the street, which led straight to the furnace under the clinic. The furnace was used to dispose of amputated limbs and other biohazardous materials from the clinic upstairs. Young Avellanal used it to dispose of the bodies of his victims. He was supposedly assisted by a mysterious unnamed nurse, who may have been one of the other girls in the bordello. It is theorized that she may have manipulated the bedeviled son of the doctor to get rid of her rivals.

It is not known whether the young man was ever brought to justice, as the police never investigated the crimes. Some people have postulated that the madame of the bordello finally found out what was going on and had the young son "taken care of" by some of her more nefarious clients. Then, she used the influential clients to cover the whole thing up.

The clinic became the Don Vicente de Ybor Historic Inn but is currently undergoing renovation. The cellar is home to a restaurant and bar area, where you can sit at a table next to the walled-up tunnel entrance. Behind this wall, the furnace is encased in stone. The ghost of the young Avellanal is still seen dragging ghostly bodies through the bar and through the wall. Sometimes he is accompanied by the mysterious nurse figure.

The bordello was eventually closed, and the building is now the property of the Church of Scientology. As the cigar factories became more and more automated, the whole area of Ybor City declined. In the 1980s, the area began to surge as an arts district and then a night spot filled with clubs and entertainment venues. Today, many of the old historical buildings are being restored, and the area is booming once again.

One of the most iconic structures in Tampa Bay is the Sulphur Springs Tower. Once part of Mave's Arcade, the first indoor shopping mall in the

The Don Vicente de Ybor Historic Inn sits on top of the infamous tunnels that once allowed bodies to be dragged to the furnace underneath. *Courtesy of author.*

United States, the tower was built to pump water from the spring to supply the residents of Tampa Bay with natural spring water. The arcade was a marvel of the early 1900s and housed many businesses.

When the Great Depression hit, the arcade and many of its businesses struggled. When a nearby dam was sabotaged by disgruntled workers, the whole arcade and the Sulphur Springs Hotel next to it were severely damaged by flooding. This was the final straw, and the arcade and hotel were soon closed. It was decades before both were finally demolished. The tower stayed in operation and continued to supply drinking water, until it was closed by the City of Tampa in the 1970s.

The ghosts of the tower are apparently the souls of those who lost everything in the flood and the Great Depression. Many business owners took their lives by jumping from the top of the tower. One spectral lady in a long, flowing, 1920s-style gown is frequently seen jumping off the tower. Since the tower is visible from I-275, there are frequent reports of people witnessing her ghost falling over and over again. With the advent of car phones and cellphones, the numbers of calls to the Tampa Police Department grew exponentially. It is now known among officers as the "Suicide Tower." There have never been any suicides officially reported at the location, and the tower is sealed off to visitors.

Downtown Tampa is home to many ghost stories, including the ghost of the doorman at the historic Tampa Theatre. Several ghosts are known to haunt the old Tampa Bay Hotel, which is now the Henry B. Plant Museum. The most famous ghost is the man himself. Henry Plant is seen walking the Riverwalk near his grand hotel with unique spires, which now is part of the University of Tampa.

NORTHERN PINELLAS

Tarpon Springs and Clearwater

The small town of Anclote is nestled on US 19 just between Holiday and the world-famous Tarpon Springs. Anclote is typical of Florida's small coastal communities. Originally home to Tocobaga Indians, and the site of one of their many burial grounds around Tampa Bay, this small town has quite a dark history.

The area was frequented by pirates who would sail safely into port and harass Tampa Bay to the south. A mass grave of slaves, who must have been slaughtered on the boat carrying them to the United States, was discovered during construction of the town's power plant. One of the lost pioneer cemeteries of Tampa Bay is believed to be located somewhere in the confines of the town—long paved and built over and lost to history.

The town was victim to fire many times, with the records building burning down twice, which has caused its early history to be spotty at best. A lot of metaphysical experts believe the area is marked as a dark portal due to historical evidence of frequent Indian clashes and so many more historical atrocities. Some mediums refuse to even visit the town.

The most famous spirit in the town is the ghost of a blonde girl named Cindy. The girl appears along Anclote Road wearing an outfit that looks like she stepped out of a music video from the '80s. She looks very badly beaten and is often seen crying. If approached, she will ask for help. This ghost is so real that many witnesses have taken her in their cars and listened to her story while looking for help. She claims she was beaten and raped by four men at the nearby Anclote Cemetery. She then vanishes without a trace.

Another ghost is often seen in the evening in the woods near the cemetery. Just before dawn, she is seen running through the woods naked, as though being chased by something unseen. This second appearance matches the description of Cindy and is thought to be the poor lost soul. The cemetery was nearly abandoned once and was so far out of the way that it became a haven for drug dealers and other criminals. Some of this might lend credence to legend of Cindy. Many folks learned to stay away from the cemetery because of its shady past, but others stayed away because of the ghosts.

Recently, as the area around the cemetery was being developed, a local group began to reclaim the cemetery from overgrowth and the bad elements that were calling it home. Now much more accessible, Anclote Cemetery is a hauntingly beautiful cemetery. Shortly after its reclamation, people began to notice one resident was not completely happy and rather enjoyed being left alone.

The restless spirit is called Jacks. He is often seen in a Union army uniform from the Civil War. He is also described as looking a lot like a young Henry Winkler of *Happy Days* fame but with a turn-of-the-twentieth-century mustache. He does not like visitors and has been known to be very aggressive. There are some reports of him physically attacking female investigators by pulling their hair or shoving them to the ground. Because the society that is restoring the cemetery does not officially allow investigations after dark, it

Is this the grave of the mysterious ghost known as "Franks" in Anclote Cemetery? *Courtesy of author.*

is hard to confirm these stories. There is a grave in the cemetery from the Jacks family, which may be the origin of the name of the vengeful spirit.

Just south of the cemetery lies a swampy wilderness area that is home to yet another ghostly Skunk Ape. Some call him the Hobo, as he is more often smelled than seen. The putrid smell of rot and decay precedes his apparition. Witnesses say they feel as though they are walking into spider webs when he begins to interact with them, though they are usually far away from trees. When seen, he appears as an impossibly large, hairy figure that hulks into view along a nearby tree line before vanishing into thin air.

Tarpon Springs is the home of a few ghostly locations, including the Retro Play Museum, which is an all-you-can-play arcade with tons of pinball machines and old video games. Staff here have reported often hearing footsteps on the upper floor when no one is up there. They also come in to see that some of the machines have turned themselves on overnight.

The old city hall, which is now the location of the Tarpon Historical Society, houses several ghosts. There have been many sightings of moving objects and dark shadowy shapes in the upper floors. The famous sponge docks have several stories of pirate ghosts and ghostly old sailors coming home after being lost at sea for decades. A shop called Getaguru claims to be on the very portal that brings such entities to the area, but we could find nothing more than an eclectic bunch of tourist memorabilia and metaphysical books there.

Down US 19 lies Rose Cemetery. Just across the street from the well-kept Cycadia Cemetery, this cemetery is nearly its exact opposite. Cycadia has manicured lawns, a designed layout and cleaned headstones. Rose Cemetery was the African American cemetery in the town and is only recently being renovated by volunteers.

Rose Cemetery is haunted by several ghostly inhabitants, mostly noted by students at the neighboring soccer field. There is also a strange legend about a man who was buried there with his bed frame. The man was homeless but was taken in near the end of his life by a local family. He was so thankful for a bed that he asked if he could be buried with it. The family honored his wishes. His bed frame was supposedly still there until recently.

Paranormal teams frequent this site to report on the hauntings and activities at Rose. Recent accounts report on the high quality of EVPs recorded here, as the area seems conducive to spirit communication. It is almost impossible to find a night when some local investigators are not looking into this location, as it is one of the few cemeteries in the area to allow night visitors.

Where Cycadia Cemetery across the road is beautiful and maintained, Rose Cemetery has only recently begun to be restored by volunteers. *Courtesy of author.*

A short drive will bring you to the Belleview Inn in Clearwater, which was once part of the sprawling Belleview-Biltmore Hotel and Spa. Built by Henry Plant in 1897 as a place to house those traveling on his rail lines, this magnificent Victorian hotel was the smaller sister to Plant's nearby Tampa Bay Hotel. Built on a thirty-five-foot bluff overlooking the Gulf of Mexico, the beautiful resort was open for many years and housed many famous guests.

As the hotel aged, it began to degrade and eventually closed. It was scheduled for demolition despite efforts by historical societies to keep the beautiful building intact. It closed for the last time in 2009. During the closing, visitors were allowed to visit the hotel one last time. Bellhops and visitors were dressed in period clothing from every century of the hotel's operation.

We went with a local paranormal team to the closing because they wanted to see the ghost on the third floor. A ghostly bellhop is often seen coming out of a room at the end of the hall at the top of the stairs. As we reached the top of the stairs, a bellhop did come out of the room at the far end of the hall. We all laughed because we had no idea the hotel would think to put an actor up there. We thought we had gone up in secret. The bellhop came down the hall toward us, and I told him he had done an amazing job scaring us. He walked past without saying a word. One of the hunters on the end turned and asked, "What are you all laughing at, and who were you talking to?"

The view of a train dropping off guests at the Belleview-Biltmore Hotel during its early days of operation. *Courtesy of St. Petersburg Museum of History.*

A body was found in the balcony of the Capitol Theatre in Clearwater during renovation. *Courtesy of author.*

The original Crabby Bill's in Clearwater Beach is built on the ruins of the previous building. The spirits of the previous building still linger on the upper floors. *Courtesy of author.*

We had just seen the ghost. A group of investigators and a historian with a camera in tow had just missed capturing a ghost on film. We feared it was the last time anyone would have the opportunity since the hotel closed the next day. The demolition ball was coming.

In 2016 a new company purchased the old building. Recently reopened as the Belleview Inn, the company has managed to restore much of the main building to its original grand design and has made it an amazing place to visit once again. We wonder if the bellhop is still there on the third floor. We've already booked our stay for later this year.

Downtown Clearwater is home to the Bilheimer Capitol Theatre, which opened in 1921. It operated for several decades before being sold to the Royalty Theater Company in 1981. During renovations, they discovered the body of a young man named Bill Neville, who had been murdered in the balcony area.

In 2009 the theater was purchased by the City of Clearwater and Ruth Eckerd Hall. These organizations revitalized and reopened it with much success. Bill's ghost is said to haunt the balcony and to frighten guests. Another ghost, known as the Captain, is often seen wearing a blue coat and sailor's cap in the hallways.

Across the bridge to Clearwater Beach is the impressive original Crabby Bill's restaurant. Crabby Bill's has several locations along the Pinellas beaches, and each has its own ghost story. The original location, though, includes a famous ghost seen by late-night workers. This spirit is often seen staring out of the top-floor window, looking out over the Gulf as the nearly nightly summer thunderstorms move off into the bay.

ST. PETERSBURG

The northwest side of Tampa Bay is covered by the Pinellas Peninsula. The bulk of this peninsula is the city of St. Petersburg and its many barrier beach towns. The city has undergone a renaissance in the past few decades. It has gone from being the retirement capital of the world to a bustling community of artists and trendy restaurants, with a booming brewing industry. With so much construction and urban renewal, many of the old historical sites are being bulldozed to make way for modern high-rise offices, expensive condos and even more trendy shops and eateries.

Legends speak of Babe Ruth and Al Capone haunting various locations throughout the city. They have become the "George Washington slept here" story of the Tampa Bay area. There is little proof that they were ever in the area for long and even less evidence to suggest their ghosts are tied to the area. Another rumor is that noted author Jack Kerouac haunts the world-famous Haslam's Book Store. While the author did frequent the area and that shop, it is unlikely that his ghost accounts for some of the poltergeist activity reported in the building.

Simply put, owners found out that tying a famous person to the ghostly inhabitant at their location in Florida meant more tourist dollars. It is far more interesting to think a famous rock star or author haunts a building than some random person. It is also much better to put on the brochures. This is why we have to be so diligent when publishing these stories.

The most famously haunted location in St. Petersburg is the Vinoy Hotel. It was built in 1925 by Aymer Vinoy Laughner as a hotel to rival those built by Henry B. Plant. It took nearly a year to build and was only open seasonally—from December to March. Many noted celebrities stayed in the hotel, including Jimmy Stewart, Calvin Coolidge, Herbert Hoover and, of course, Babe Ruth and Al Capone. During World War II, the hotel was commandeered by the United States Army and used as a training school for officers. It reopened to guests shortly after the war but began a decline that led to its closure in 1974. It sat abandoned for more than a decade.

In the early 1990s, it was purchased and remodeled with nearly $100 million in renovation costs. It is now a four-star hotel owned by Bryan Glazer, who also owns the Tampa Bay Buccaneers NFL team. The pink hotel stands proudly near the St. Petersburg Municipal Marina.

Through the years, many ghosts and supernatural experiences have been reported in the hotel. One of the players of the visiting Pittsburgh Pirates baseball team had an encounter with a translucent man standing at the desk in his room late one night. He was so scared that he insisted the team be moved from the hotel the next day. Major League Baseball does not allow visiting teams to be hosted at the Vinoy Hotel anymore. It is an actual rule.

Paranormal teams have frequently investigated the hotel. The famous *Ghost Hunters* television show did a special episode and uncovered some strange activity that still has not been debunked.

One of the strangest haunted locations anywhere in the world lies just down the road from the Vinoy. It sits on the way to the landing of the old St. Petersburg Pier area, which is currently being remodeled. It is next door to the wonderful St. Petersburg Museum of History, where we do a lot of our historical research. It is a grand brick octagonal building that is also a bathroom. Comfort Station One was designed by the same architect who made St. Mary's Church and the Vinoy, and it has a similar style to its grand sister buildings. It opened to worldwide press in 1927. Do you know any other restrooms that have opened to renowned acclaim?

A legend says that the architect was never paid for St. Mary's, so he built the bathroom to look like the church in jest. In truth, the bathroom was opened first. The architect used it to practice techniques he would later use in the design of St. Mary's.

However, there is a dark presence in this bathroom and homeless people in St. Petersburg will almost never go anywhere near it. At night, voices are often heard in some sort of heated argument. Later, a woman will be heard screaming from inside. Upon inspection, there is never anyone to be seen inside.

Another grand pink hotel stands on the opposite side of the peninsula. It is also a noted haunted location. The Don CeSar Hotel was built in the mid-1920s—just like the Vinoy. Thomas Rowe built the large pink palace as a tribute to his lost love—an opera singer named Lucinda.

The couple apparently met in secret in London, as she was the star of the opera *Maritana*. When her parents found out about their burgeoning romance, they forced her to return to Spain. Rowe sent many letters, but they were all returned unopened after being refused by her parents. He received one letter from her in which he discovered she had died. The letter included that she was sad he never wrote her, but she would wait for him by their fountain forever.

Rowe built the magnificent hotel and called it the Don CeSar after one of the main characters of *Maritana*. He built a replica of the fountain where he and his love met in London, in hopes her spirit would find him.

The hotel boomed even during the Great Depression, but it was seized by the military during World War II and used as a hospital. When it was finally returned to the owners, extensive remodeling had to be done. In the mid-1970s, people began to notice the hauntings. A man with a Panama hat is often seen and is thought to be the ghost of Rowe. People often see sailors and military nurses walking the hallways at night. The fifth floor is supposedly the most haunted location and has been the site of many sightings of figures in the night and strange sounds echoing through the halls.

There are many other haunted locations throughout the peninsula and its beachfront communities. Just remember, not every ghost here is Babe Ruth, Jack Kerouac or Al Capone.

SOUTH OF THE BAY

Bradenton and Sarasota

J ust over the haunted Sunshine Skyway Bridge is Bradenton. Founded in 1842, the city gets its name from Doctor Joseph Braden. Braden moved to the area and built a giant plantation house out of tabby. It resembled the styles of forts built by the Spanish, so it got the nickname of Braden Castle.

Dr. Braden and his brother had purchased the land here with their friend Robert Gamble, and their slaves built the house. The walls were twenty inches thick from the poured lime and shell mix. Each floor of the grand house had a long breezeway down the middle to help cool the building. Their plantation became one of the largest sugar plantations in Florida and eventually encompassed more than one thousand acres. Many cabins and buildings were built to house the families and slaves who worked on the farm.

In 1856 the plantation was attacked by a local Native American tribe. The thick walls of the mansion provided an excellent defense. The raiders decided to attack the outlying cabins deeper into the plantation when they realized the main house was too well defended. In all, the Bradens lost a few valuables, some cabins were damaged and several workers and slaves were killed, though even more were kidnapped. The raiding party was tracked down and slain, and much was returned to the plantation. The house was now called Braden Castle due to its imposing appearance and surviving the attack.

The family fell on financial hard times and the plantation was foreclosed upon by 1857. By the mid-1860s, the house was mostly out

These tabby ruins are all that remain of what was once known as Braden Castle. *Courtesy of author.*

of residential use and had become a town meeting area and park. The house began to fall into disrepair, and ultimately, a large fire engulfed the wood-shingle roof in 1903.

Braden Castle is now a pile of ruins surrounded by a chain link fence by the Braden Castle Retirement Community. The stone and tabby walls lie broken around the old plot overlooking the long pier and park between the buildings and the river. It is a tranquil place in this nestled community, where 90 percent of the population is only here for three to five months of the winter.

Some people say the castle has never truly been empty. While building the house, a shopkeeper from the town died and numerous slaves died from yellow fever and other diseases. Then there was all the turmoil during the Third Seminole War, of which the raid was just a small part. Stories of the ghosts of the ruins date back as far as the 1860s, when couples would go to the castle for a romantic getaway—far away from prying eyes. In the 1920s, the Tin-Can Tourists, a mutual aid society, began to travel to Florida in droves to camp, and they often stayed in the park near the ruins. Many of them reported unusual sounds coming from the castle walls.

Several ghost hunters came to the castle ruins in the late 1970s. Deciding to see if this could be the next Amityville, they went past the walls when they heard strange noises and odd knocking sounds. One member of the team heard what sounded like a baby crying and ran to investigate. He was startled when he was knocked flat by a stray goat that had decided to hide among the ruins.

Today, folks in the community tend to say the castle is a curiosity and little more than a point of interest on the map. The park is a shady place to walk their pets. Most admit that they don't go by the castle after dark. There are screams and the sounds of battle heard on some evenings. Dark shadows also stalk the ruins of Braden Castle.

Richard Gamble, Braden's friend, also purchased some land not too far from the castle. In the town of Eustis, he built his own plantation. For his home on the sprawling plantation, he built a large antebellum manor house—again made primarily from tabby. It is the only surviving plantation house in the Florida Peninsula.

During the Civil War the house was the headquarters for Captain Archibald McNeil. This famous Confederate blockade runner eluded Union forces throughout the war. His ships sailed out of the nearby river and harassed the ports of Tampa, Sarasota and others along the Gulf Coast. He even managed to get supplies in and out of New Orleans. Toward the end of the war, Confederate secretary of state Judah P. Benjamin fled to the Gamble Mansion for refuge. Captain McNeil even assisted him in fleeing from Union forces following the defeat of the Confederacy. Benjamin had been accused of helping plan the assassination of President Abraham Lincoln. Fearing no fair trial, he fled with McNeil to Europe.

Gamble's sugar mill was destroyed by Union raiders in 1864. The ruins show that it must have been one of the largest of its time. It lies

The Gamble Plantation in Bradenton is the only pre–Civil War plantation still standing on Florida's Gulf Coast. *Courtesy of author.*

about half a mile north of the Gamble Mansion. The State of Florida acquired the property of the mill and the plantation, and they are now a state park. The state is trying to deflect some of the harsh history of slavery and the Confederate leanings of the mansion to try to shift the park into more of a natural history park. Archaeologists are stationed on the site to learn more about the natives of the land and even to inspect some prehistoric fossils.

The ghosts at the mansion have different ideas, though. There is an evil and wrathful spirit here that many believe to be David Lanner, the former overseer of the plantation. Known for being a harsh master, it is said he was brutal to the field slaves and their families. In death he has apparently gotten even angrier. Volunteers at the mansion have said they hear heavy footsteps on the wooden floors when he approaches. They are then shoved or knocked out of the way by an invisible force. Muffled arguments, followed by bellowing shouts, come from the grounds and end with the echoing crack of a whip. Some people claim to hear gunfire and hoofbeats echoing across the park at all hours.

The Bali Hai Resort on Bradenton Beach is the home to a ghostly bride walking the beach behind the hotel. *Courtesy of author.*

On Bradenton Beach is the wonderful Bali Hai Beach Resort. The ghost here is of a lonely bride who walks the beach behind the resort. She looks longingly out to sea—as if searching for her lost husband. For some reason, this ghost is reported to be witnessed more often in August than at any other time of the year. The mystery of who she was remains to this day.

Nearby, Coquina Beach Park at the end of Anna Maria Island once held a small hotel. The hotel is long gone, but the land is now a picnic area right next to the beach. A shadowy specter has been seen leaving what used to be the hotel and walking toward the beach. This ghost has been observed so many times that there is a dedicated watch group that keeps records of his appearances and updates its webpage weekly.

Another notable haunted location in the area is the Hampton Inn and Suites in downtown Bradenton. Currently under renovation, workers claim that this 1920s hotel is rife with paranormal activity—tools go missing and break, weird noises echo through abandoned halls and full apparitions have caused more than a few crew members to turn in their notices. The hotel is partially open, but we are eagerly waiting to explore the ghosts on the upper floors even further.

Lastly, before you head south, you might want to stop and have dinner at the Island Time Bar and Grill on Bradenton Beach. The old building is home to many ghostly presences that date back to when it was the Sun House Restaurant. The upstairs dining room has a strange mist-like ghost that appears in the late evenings, according to workers. One waitress claims to have heard arguing outside the office one night, but when she went to visit, no one was there.

Farther south is the wonderful city of Sarasota. The landlocked Sarasota Bay has an amazing ghostly story that we discussed in *Eerie Florida*. It involves the daughter of Henando de Soto and a young Native American chief and is well worth perusing when you get the chance.

The city is famous for being the winter home of the Ringling Bros. Circus until their final performance in 2017. For 146 years, the circus came to this town and left a lasting impression on Florida. To this day, other circuses still call the area home, but none is quite as successful as Ringling Bros.

John Ringling was one of the four brothers who owned "The Greatest Show on Earth" and had done well for his family. In the 1920s, they decided to build their palatial home on the shores of Sarasota Bay. The Ca' d'Zan, or "House of John" from the Venetian dialect, was built by architect Dwight James Baum. The house is one of the last gilded mansions of its era. While traveling with the circus, John and his wife, Mable, amassed a large collection of art. A short distance away from their home, they built the palatial Ringling Museum of Art and opened it to the public.

They only lived there a short while before they both passed away. Their ghosts are often seen wandering their gardens hand in hand. Sometimes they are seen on the veranda overlooking the bay from the Ca' d'Zan. Though most tours of the grounds try to hide it, they are both buried in a small rose garden just off the path to the big house. They are one of the few exceptions, and we do think the most famous people associated with the house are the ghosts in question.

THE EVERGLADES

Everglades City and Flight 401

There are more than three million acres of untamed land that the native Miccosukee tribe calls Pa-hay-okee. This land is known to the world as the Everglades. While the name conjures up the images of swamps and wetlands, the area is truly composed of many interlinked ecosystems, including cypress swamps, sawgrass marsh, rocky islands, the marine ecosystem and tropical hardwood forests. It is home to many thousands of forms of wildlife—some native and many invasive—that are thriving here. It is also the home of murders, mysteries, monsters and more unusual phenomena—both natural and supernatural.

Near the end of the nineteenth century, a settlement on the edge of the Ten Thousand Islands was formed on the isolated Chokoloskee Island. It stood twenty feet above sea level thanks to thousands of years of occupation by the Native Americans of the Glades culture, who raised the terrain with shell middens.

Chokoloskee Island was isolated and home to only the hardiest settlers and those who didn't want to be found. It was nearly impossible to reach except by boat. It was a place for fugitives and criminals, and others of their ilk, to lay low from law enforcement groups or rivals who might have a price on their heads. The community of settlers tended to be wary of newcomers for this very reason.

One such man came to the island in the mid-1880s. He was notorious outlaw Edgar Watson. Originally from South Carolina, Watson went to the town to raise sugar, hunt and kill alligators. He built his home on one of the shell middens on a nearby island. He frequently traveled to the trading post in town, called the Smallwood Store, to sell the fruits of his farming and hunting.

Watson always seemed to be on edge, according to his fellow settlers, as though he was always looking over his shoulder. Rumors began that he had shot and killed outlaw Belle Star before fleeing to this area. Word got out about a drunken fight that Watson had won that ended with his rival dead and dumped into the alligator-infested waters. People tended to give Watson a wide berth in the small island community.

Watson's cane plantation began to prosper. Despite his reputation, his bottled cane syrup had made him a rich man. His eccentricities were suddenly ignored by the town, and people wanted to be friends with the rich man. Then he got into a fight with another landowner in the area named Adolphus Santini. The argument got heated and ended when Watson pulled out his knife and slit Santini's throat. The victim survived the attack, and Watson was never arrested nor charged. There were rumors of Santini being paid a large sum by Watson to not press charges.

Watson also always seemed to have plenty of migrant workers on his farm, despite the harsh and brutal conditions of the Everglades. When the harvest came in, Watson would come into town, and many would note that most of his labor force had gone away. Watson would boast that he had paid them all so well that they all left the area. This led to even more workers clamoring to work for him.

Rumors began to spread, though, that he hadn't paid the workers—he had killed them and hid the bodies in the swamps that surrounded his plantation. This rumor began to gain foothold in the minds of the locals. When someone would leave the area at the end of harvest season, people

The view of the islands from the back of the Smallwood Store. Watson's Island was not far to the north. *Courtesy of author.*

began to speculate if the person had received what they referred to as a "Watson Payday."

When bones and full skeletons started turning up in lands around his property, Watson claimed they were simply the bones of the Native Americans who used to inhabit the area. With no way to disprove it, again he went unpunished or investigated.

Watson bought a neighboring island and tried to evict the family who had been homesteading on it. They refused to leave and told him they were going to wire to the local marshal to assist. When the family was found dead on the island a few days later, Watson blamed the attack on outlaws hiding in the swamp.

In 1910 some fishermen spotted something odd in the water near Watson's property. When they saw the flowing golden hair and the dead face of poor Hannah Smith, the rumors were no longer going to be easily dismissed. The poor girl had been slashed open and tied to a rock in the water. She had been in the employ of Edgar Watson. Within days, another plantation worker named Dutchy Melvin was also discovered dead on the property. The town was convinced that Watson was a serial killer. A former worker came forward and claimed to have witnessed Watson killing several people over the years, and he was terrified he'd be next for talking.

Watson was confronted with these allegations. He proclaimed his innocence and blamed the deaths on a noted outlaw who had been seen in the region, Leslie Cox. To carry out this charade, he went to nearby Fort Myers to ask the local sheriff to make him a deputy. He wanted to hunt down Cox himself. His request was denied.

When a strong hurricane came into the area later that year, the small community was in an uproar. When the storm passed, Watson said he was finally going to go hunt down Cox and make him pay. He went to the Smallwood Store to see the owner, Ted Smallwood, and his wife. He wanted ammo for his shotgun and pistol. There are rumors that the Smallwoods sold him waterlogged ammo on purpose.

Watson came back to town with a hat filled with holes. He claimed he had tracked down Cox and shot him. He was met by an angry mob. When asked where the body was, Watson claimed the flooded river had taken it. When Watson saw they weren't buying it, he pulled his gun. It didn't fire because of the wet ammunition. Members of the mob fired their guns. Watson's body was dragged through the swamp at Rabbit Key, where he was buried. When the sheriff was told and came to examine the body, Watson was discovered to have thirty-three gunshot wounds.

The Smallwood Store still stands today. It is now a museum and is much easier to get to, thanks to a causeway built to Everglades City in 1954. There, you can see relics of the old outpost. It even includes a section dedicated to Edgar Watson and his brutal end. The store is said to hold the ghost of Watson and the echoes of all the shots. You can canoe or kayak to his old plantation island, where the buildings are all gone. You can still see the well and some structural foundations. No one likes to stay after dark—mostly because of mosquitoes and alligators, but some say Watson still protects his land.

The murders have never truly been solved. Did Watson really do it? Was he framed by rivals? Was there really a Leslie Cox?

Mysterious deaths and corpses are still found in the Everglades. There are currently more than 180 unsolved homicides in the Everglades. Bodies of murder victims were often found in the '70s and '80s. Due to the size of the area, the natural predators and the density of the swamps, officials believe that for every body found, there are probably two more that haven't been found. On average, there are more than 400 missing person cases a year in Collier County, which contains a good portion of the Everglades. People just seem to vanish here.

There are also many ghost stories tied to these murders. The area is home to a lost city a few miles south of Alligator Alley. Once a thriving Seminole Indian village, it was abandoned seemingly overnight. The shelters and buildings have rotted over time, but there are artifacts here that are more than a thousand years old. Called Ghost City, it sits in a particularly thick forest of pine trees. Legends of the site state that Confederate soldiers once fled here and hid a stash of gold. While they slept, they were attacked by the ghostly tribe members coming to protect their sacred land from the intruders. Several soldiers were killed, and the few survivors told the tale. Ghost City is a protected archaeological site, and many boat tours will not go to it.

Another famous ghost story in the Everglades is that of the lost ship. A group of pirates on the Gulf Coast had just plundered a Spanish caravel. The pirate captain was determined to make a name for himself, so he refused to keep any prisoners alive and released one. He let the Spanish crew decide who would be let go. The daughter of the caravel's captain was selected to live.

The pirates loved this idea and slew the captured crew. When the girl was the only one left, they told her that while they were going to let her live, they weren't going to let her go. She ran to the edge of the ship and leapt overboard rather than being mistreated or defiled by the pirates. As she leapt to the sea, she prayed that God would never find mercy on these pirates. When she hit the water, a large tidal wave crashed from the otherwise calm sea and sank the ship to the bottom of the ocean, which was now dry. When the waters came back in force, the second wave launched the boat high into the air and deep into the murky waters of the Everglades.

The ship was lost in the endless rivers and swamps of the Everglades. The pirates are damned to an eternity of sailing the swamps until they could find their way out to open ocean again. On dark nights when the moon is out, the legend says you may see a strange mossy green glow as the ghostly ship and its undead crew sail away in search of a path to the Gulf.

One of the most famous ghost stories in Florida begins in the Everglades. It started with the tragic crash of Eastern Air Lines Flight 401. Pilot Bob Loft, who had more than three decades of flight experience, led the crew of the Lockheed L-1011-1 Tristar on that fateful trip on December 29, 1972. The flight was returning to Miami International Airport from New York City. The crew included First Officer Albert John Stockstill, Flight Engineer Donald Louis Repo and ten flight attendants on the widebody aircraft.

The plane began its descent and the passengers and crew prepared for landing. Stockstill noticed that the landing gear indicator light had not turned on to show the nose gear was down and locked for landing. They tried cycling the landing gear several times and were put into a holding pattern over the Everglades to see if there could be a way to fix it. The cruising altitude of the pattern was just above two thousand feet.

The plane was put into autopilot while the crew attempted to repair the light, and Repo climbed down into the "hell hole." The hell hole is a way to check systems while in flight under the cockpit. It is hot and cramped and earned its nickname. There was a small porthole that could be used to visually confirm if the landing gear was down, but it was an involved process and took some time to crawl and reach.

It is estimated that at this point someone disabled the autopilot on accident, while working on the landing gear button. The distraction—and the sheer darkness and vastness of the Everglades—kept the crew from realizing just how low their altitude was dropping.

Repo had crawled to the porthole and saw the gear was down, but he also saw the treetops. He called out to the startled cockpit crew, but it was far too late. The plane crashed into the swamp at 227 miles per hour and ripped itself apart. Flames and jet fuel filled the Everglades. Stockstill was killed instantly. Robert Loft, the pilot, died while being extracted from the burning wreckage. Don Repo survived for a time but later died in the hospital from his injuries. In all, 97 of the 163 passengers died, as well as 2 of the 10 attendants. It was the second-deadliest single-aircraft disaster in the United States at the time.

A short time later, the crews and passengers of other Eastern L-1011 Tristar flights began to report seeing unusual sightings of an Eastern Airlines pilot while aboard their ships. Some of the crew members on these ships recognized the long-dead Robert Loft. One of the surviving stewardesses had an encounter on another flight when she swore Don Repo in his flight engineer uniform was fixing an oven in the galley.

Both of the men were seen quite often on other flights, walking the aisles and talking to passengers before flights. One woman saw an airline officer sitting next to her who looked pale and unresponsive. When she called for an attendant to check on him, he vanished in front of her and several other passengers. The passenger had to be restrained by other passengers and crew to be calmed down. Later, one of the attendants showed her a picture of the crew of Flight 401, and she pointed out that the man had been Don Repo.

One sighting of Loft scared a crew so badly that the flight had to be cancelled. Once, a crew heard a strange knocking sound coming from the hell hole under the cockpit. Fearing a mechanical problem, the flight engineer went to look and screamed when he opened the door. His old and long-dead friend Don Repo was hunched there, looking at him. When he disappeared and the engineer calmed down, he went down and found an active fault that might have jeopardized the crew and flight.

Eastern Airlines began to pull all of the logbooks with these incidents and start fresh ones. Crews that reported sightings were sent for psychological evaluations and were suspended. Crew members stopped reporting the apparitions for fear of losing their jobs. The ghost kept appearing, though.

Repo appeared in the galley of another flight and startled an attendant. She called for the captain, and several crew members came and witnessed the apparition—including the flight engineer. This engineer had known Don Repo and recognized him immediately. Repo turned to him and said, "You should watch out for fire on this plane." He vanished in the blink of an eye. The plane had a severe engine fire and had to perform an emergency landing.

While the airline was having all sorts of issues with the ghosts, the vice president of Eastern Airlines began a conversation with an officer while sitting in first class on a flight. It took him a few minutes to realize that he was not talking to the captain of his flight but was talking to Robert Loft. Then, the ghostly pilot vanished.

Famously, Loft appeared in a cockpit on one flight and said to the crew, "There will never be another crash. We won't let it happen."

Another crew saw Repo while they were doing their preflight check, and Repo said, "Don't worry. I've already done it."

Interestingly, the ghosts were never seen on the same flight, though they were both seen many times by multiple witnesses. They were never described as anything other than solid and real. Many witnesses had not even realized they were interacting with ghosts.

Eastern Airlines began to puzzle out that the ghosts only appeared on planes that had received some of the undamaged salvaged parts from Flight 401. The Flight Safety Foundation received so many reports from the witnesses that they issued a report to Eastern Airlines stating, "The reports were given by experienced and trustworthy pilots and crew. We consider them to be significant."

Eastern Airlines CEO and former astronaut Frank Borman said the rumors and stories were "garbage." The federal report was dismissed. The company denied the sightings and refused any further investigations of the incidents. What no one knew was that they were quietly removing all the parts of Flight 401 from every plane that had received them. Once they were removed, the sightings ceased. The ghosts of Flight 401 have become one of the most important talking points when paranormal investigators try to show proof of life after death. The story of Flight 401 has been made into television shows, songs and movies.

The evidence is compelling. The eyewitness reports were made by high-ranking, experienced officers and crew, and passenger witnesses could have had no previous knowledge of the other incidents. Reports were still filed, even with the threat of crew members losing their jobs. Despite these accounts, there is still not one solid shred of physical evidence. There is still no real answer as to what happened on all these other flights.

The crash site itself is still very active with ghostly phenomena and is investigated frequently by those willing to brave the swamps of the Everglades. Lesser known than the ghosts of the flight are the disembodied screams and strange temperature spikes and drops at the site. Shadowy figures are also seen hiding in the darkness. The faces of drowned figures sometimes seem to float up and vanish in the water at the site.

In May 1996, just a few hundred yards away from the crash site of Flight 401, another plane crashed into the Everglades. ValuJet Flight 592 crashed into the same marsh, killing all 110 passengers and crew on board.

A few miles south, a memorial was placed off Alligator Alley for the crash of Flight 592. Since there is still no marker for Flight 401, many also use this structure as a marker for that crash. It seems to be more than a coincidence that there have been two horrific crashes less than a few hundred yards from each other deep in the Florida Everglades.

SOUTHEAST FLORIDA

Palm Beach, Lake Worth, Delray Beach and Boca Raton

One of the chief contenders for the most haunted house in Florida is in the town of West Palm Beach. Originally located at 327 Aracia Street, this impressive Victorian "Painted Lady" house was built by construction workers from Henry Flagler's hotels in 1906. It was built to house the caretakers of the Woodlawn Cemetery, which was just across the road. It became known as the "Gatekeeper's House."

The caretakers were meant to help maintain the graveyard and to keep an eye out for grave robbers or vandals. A short time after its construction, the house began to be used as a funeral parlor due to its proximity to the cemetery. One of the workers at the funeral home was a man known as Buck.

Local stories claim that Buck was a very large man who liked to go over to the taverns near the cemetery and enjoy a drink or two. One night he got into a heated argument with someone at the bar, and he was killed. His ghost is seen walking the porch and the grounds of the house quite often.

In the mid-1920s, the first city manager and superintendent of public works for the City of West Palm Beach was offered the Gatekeeper's House as his new residence. Karl Riddle was thrilled to gain such a lovely home in addition to his new appointment. He hired several workers to update the house and make it more livable, as it would no longer be a funeral parlor. Riddle agreed to oversee the cemetery for the city as part of getting the house.

When the Great Depression hit, one of Riddle's employees, Jonathan, became despondent over his financial situation. Seeing no other way out, he climbed up the stairs to the attic. He tied a rope to a central beam and hanged himself. Riddle had the body prepared and sent other workers into the attic to remove the beam.

After the suicide, Riddle's diary began to recount how difficult it was to keep staff in the home. Workers began to report strange and unusual occurrences and would quit suddenly. One report even included claims of clanging chains in the attic. Riddle and his family moved out shortly thereafter, and the house sat empty for many years.

Several businesses tried to return the building to some semblance of its former glory over the years, but none of the occupants lasted more than a year. It was even used as a women's dormitory building for students at nearby Palm Beach Atlantic College for a time. By 1980, it had stood empty for some time and was scheduled for demolition.

The city decided to try to donate the house to John Riddle, the nephew of Karl. He in turn donated the house to the City of West Palm Beach Historical Society. The historical society agreed to preserve the house and had it dismantled and rebuilt at Yesteryear Village, which is next to the fairgrounds. It is still there on permanent display.

While being rebuilt, the supernatural activity surrounding the house began immediately. Workers would find their tools thrown downstairs from the top floor. Windows were found broken from the inside several times. Construction ground to a halt for several months as the carpenters refused to continue working on what was now known as the "Riddle House."

When it was finally restored, there was a grand reopening at Yesteryear Village. Like the Belleview-Biltmore in Clearwater, two of the guests at the reopening were in period garments. The young couple were very impressive. The historical society thought these guests were the hit of the event. When they discovered they hadn't hired anyone to do this and they didn't match any of the members who had been invited to the exclusive event, members of the historical society approached them to see where they came from. The couple vanished into thin air.

The Riddle House was made world-famous after an investigation by the *Ghost Adventures* television show on the Travel Channel. The team had encounters with Jonathan Riddle and Buck. There are many investigations at the house, and the historical society leads tours for a modest donation to help preserve all the buildings at Yesteryear Village.

Employees of the grounds have plenty of stories to tell, including a mannequin being seen in the attic window, though no such mannequin exists. Security guards have reported lights going on and off at all hours, though the house is empty. One investigative team's members encountered a poltergeist at the house and were struck by thrown objects before they even got into the house. No one is quite sure who all these ghosts are. The Riddle House certainly lives up to its name.

Across town, on Palm Beach, is the home of a man we have mentioned many times, Henry Flagler. One of the wealthiest men in the world, thanks to being one of the founders of Standard Oil, Flagler and his wife, Mary Lily, built the mansion of their dreams and called it Whitehall. Construction started in 1900 and was completed in 1902. Whitehall was to be their winter home, and he gave it to his new wife as a wedding present. They would travel here every year in a private railcar, usually No. 91.

In 1913 Henry Flagler fell down the steps at Whitehall. He was eighty-three years old and died of complications from his injuries. Mary Lily died in the home just four years later. Their niece inherited the house and quickly sold it. A ten-story office complex was built on top of a portion of the building. It was later abandoned and was destined for the wrecking ball. In 1959 one of Flagler's granddaughters saved the mansion and had it restored. The add-on was demolished. A foundation was set up to continue the maintenance of the property. The ghosts were quite thankful.

Flagler and his wife are seen on the property quite often. There are other unnamed ghosts that are seen, usually in 1920s outfits. Some people believe these ghosts to be some of Flagler's notorious mistresses. This seems unlikely. By all accounts, he had slowed down in his old age and loved his new wife. Some visitors say they see a murdered guest lying in a shadow, as though killed by an unseen hand. A famous sighting with numerous witnesses was when a tour group saw a bishop blessing a room, then saw him disappear.

While the director of Whitehall likes to disavow ghostly happenings at Whitehall, there are many volunteers and groundskeepers willing to share stories.

Farther south, you'll hit Lake Worth. This fun, artistic-leaning beach town is full of eclectic stores and trendy bars. It is also home to the Lake Worth Playhouse, which was originally built as the Oakley Theatre by two brothers, Lucien and Clarence Oakley. The brothers spent a fortune to open their dream movie house, hoping to cash in on the booming Florida tourism. They showed a silent film, accompanied by a $10,000 pipe organ, on their opening night. It was a smash hit in 1924.

When a hurricane came through in 1928 and demolished the theater, the brothers had it rebuilt. Sadly, the Great Depression hit hard in Lake Worth. Though they reopened the theater in 1929, the brothers lost

The Lake Worth Playhouse is haunted by the ghosts of its original builders. *Courtesy of author.*

ownership of the by the early 1930s. The theater was passed around for years—even showing adult films with one owner. It was finally purchased by the Lake Worth Playhouse in 1975 and restored. The nonprofit that runs the playhouse hosts many performances throughout the year.

Lucien and Clarence are thought to enjoy the shows and are frequently seen here. Their ghosts have appeared to theater patrons over and over again. Paranormal groups have had lots of luck with spirit boxes and other communication experiments at this location.

The former city hall of the beach town of Boca Raton was built in 1926 and is a marvel to behold. Its shining gold dome certainly makes the building stand out. It is now the Boca Raton History Museum, and the staff here has reported hearing an antique telephone ringing in one of the exhibits, though it is not connected to any phone lines. There are also strange voices heard throughout the old city hall.

Following the rail line south, you'll come to Delray Beach. This town is home to numerous hauntings and has a connection to Jack the Ripper.

First is the old livery station across from the old train depot from Flagler's line. This livery station has had two floors added above it. The upper floors

The Boca Raton History Museum was once the town's city hall. *Courtesy of author.*

now house the bar of the Silverball Museum. This arcade is filled with one of the largest collections of classic and modern pinball machines in the world and features machines from as far back as the 1930s.

The ghosts, though, predate the machines by about forty years. The old livery station was home to a hanging performed by a United States marshal after he apprehended a fugitive at the train depot. The ghost of the criminal is said to haunt the building. Several employees claim to not enjoy being in the building alone after dark. One bartender told us about the machines sounding like they were being jostled after everyone else had gone home. Come for the great pinball but stay for the ghost.

The Colony Hotel was built in 1926. The hotel still includes the original telephone switchboard, a complete set of Fixx Reed wicker furniture and the staff-operated elevator. Its sister hotel in Kennebunkport, Maine, housed some of the artifacts for a time, but they have been returned to their rightful home. The hotel is said to house several ghosts that still mingle under the wrought-iron lobby chandeliers. Later in the day, this crowd of spirits can be heard waltzing in the empty ballroom. It is an impressive, historic hotel and well worth paying a visit.

The Colony Hotel is quite the landmark in Palm Beach. *Courtesy of author.*

The nearby Delray Beach Playhouse is yet another haunted theater. The ghost of founder Bob Blake is seen here, checking up on the place. He usually slams doors when storms are coming close to the theater. He seems to be making sure his theater is still running smoothly. The players and staff say he's not haunting the building but looking after it.

Across town, on Atlantic Avenue, is the Blue Anchor British Pub. It looks slightly out of place in the beach community. That's because it was actually built in the Whitechapel area of London in 1846. The front of the pub and many of its fixtures were shipped brick by brick "across the pond" to the United States in the mid-1990s.

It had stood on Chancery Lane in London for more than 150 years. It had been abandoned and was about to be destroyed. Among its visitors over the years were Winston Churchill and Queen Elizabeth II. Two of the victims of Jack the Ripper had their last meals at the pub, and it is likely the killer had spent some time in the establishment.

The ghosts of the pub came with it. A woman named Bertha Starkey was killed by her husband one night at the pub. Her husband had caught her in the arms of another man after coming home early from a sea voyage. Her ghost is said to still haunt the pub. There are many accounts, including mediums and psychics who have talked to Bertha, to back up the claims of the pub.

People say some other souls reside in the pub as well. Perhaps the Ripper victims still hang about the place, but no one is afraid of the spirits. Bertha's story is even on the back of the menu. It is yet another great haunted place to enjoy in Delray Beach.

THE BERMUDA TRIANGLE

The disappearance of Flight 19 is one of the most famous in the Bermuda Triangle. It was often called the "Lost Patrol," but that is a misnomer. Flight 19 was the code name for five Grumman TBM Avenger torpedo bomber planes that had taken off for a training bomber run from the Naval Air Station at Fort Lauderdale. It was a balmy day with a light breeze and a chance of storms later that evening. This was the nineteenth training flight that day, and there was no patrol.

The flight never returned. The navy's final report on their disappearance cited "reasons unknown" as the cause of the disappearance. The five TBM Avengers were being led by the experienced commander Charles Taylor. The planes were each three-seaters and were designed to sink enemy submarines. Though World War II had ended shortly before, the planes were still in use.

There were thirteen trainees on the five planes, and Taylor was the only experienced pilot. This was to be their last training run before graduating. On December 5, 1945, just after 2:00 p.m., the planes took off for their training exercise into the clear Florida sky.

They headed east into the Atlantic to pass the Hen and Chickens Shoals of Bermuda to practice their bombing run. Then, they were to go farther east to the Bahamas. They would head north for a short run and finally head straight back to the station in Fort Lauderdale. They had done this training exercise several times before.

At about 3:30 p.m., Taylor contacted the control tower and complained that his compass was malfunctioning. He thought they had flown the

The planes of Flight 19 fly into oblivion. *Illustration by Kari Schultz.*

wrong way and were now much farther south and possibly over the Florida Keys. He felt they had been flying south instead of east. The tower told them to turn north and find Miami but only if they were sure they were over the Keys. Some people believe he had flown east all along, which would mean turning north would lead his training group deep over the Atlantic and out to sea.

By 3:45 p.m., Taylor came back over the radio sounding worried and confused. "Cannot see land, we seem to be off course," he said.

A student pilot came on. "If we could fly west, we would get home."

Using only the tools of World War II–era technology made finding their exact location difficult. The flight was most certainly lost.

At 4:45 p.m., Taylor handed over command of the mission to his second in command. There were reports that he was asked to do this by the tower, but there are no official records of that. The flight was picked up on radar at 5:50 p.m. They were just off the coast of New Smyrna Beach. Communications were so poor that they could not get this information to Flight 19.

The clear weather from the morning had now turned into a squall line of storms. The crew's communications were sporadic and sounded more desperate as their situation continued to worsen.

Two Martin Mariner sea planes were launched for search and rescue. These planes could land at sea and get the downed crew, which would surely run out of fuel. Hope was dwindling, but the rescue planes could save their lives. They headed toward the area of radar contact to begin looking for the lost training planes.

One of those rescue planes was never seen again. The last transmission from Flight 19 was at 7:04 p.m. The search plane's last transmission was at 7:27 p.m. and sounded normal. The second search plane reported seeing a ball of fire like an explosion in the sky. We still are unsure of what happened to these planes.

FORT LAUDERDALE

Fort Lauderdale has been inhabited for more than four thousand years. The original inhabitants seemed to be transitional and seasonal for the most part. It was only after the Tequesta Indians settled in the area that it seemed to stay populated for a length of time. As archaeological evidence suggests, this tribe stayed here for hundreds of years. It wasn't until the late 1890s, when trains finally made their way to the area, when the current development of the lands came about.

Originally called the New River Settlement, the East Coast Railroad brought in tons of workers and many immigrants. The Florida land boom of the 1920s caused a population explosion in the area.

In 1905 the New River Inn was built on the railway to host visitors to the city and its new fort. It had been commissioned by Nathan Bryan, a United States senator from Jacksonville. As one of the earliest hotels in the area, it did a booming business. It had all the latest amenities, including a sewage system and running water. It was even lit by the new carbide lamps.

Now it is owned by the Fort Lauderdale Historical Society. It sits in the Old Fort Lauderdale Village and hosts many exhibits on the history of the early settlers to Fort Lauderdale. The curators will also tell you all about the ghosts of the New River Inn.

These stories include a little girl who plays on the porch out front. She will play sing-song games and seems to be skittish around male ghost hunters. A man in a long, black coat and cowboy hat has been seen on the upstairs veranda. He appears to have glowing red eyes and a rifle slung over his

New River Inn is now a museum and home to several ghosts. *Courtesy of author.*

shoulder. Police have been called when it looked like he had pulled the rifle and was going to shoot a tourist walking by the inn.

Both sides of the inn are flanked by two more haunted locations. On one side is the King-Cromartie House, which was built it 1907. The wood used to build the house was mostly taken from nearby shipwrecks. The house was moved by barge to the Old Fort Lauderdale Village. The ghosts, though, seem to be from the building that stood on the grounds before—the old schoolhouse.

The schoolhouse burned down long before the King-Cromartie House was moved to the site. Now in the house, there are often the sounds of children playing. The doll room upstairs is particularly loved by investigators for its nearly consistent level of paranormal activity. The ghosts of the burned-out school seem to love the toy dolls.

The far side of the New River Inn is the home of the River House. Thomas and Reed Bryan built two homes next to each other in the early 1900s, and sometime during the 1920s, they combined the two homes and converted it into a restaurant. It was owned by descendants of the Bryan family until the late 1970s. The ghost seen here is a mischievous little boy. He likes to knock over chairs and make a mess of recently cleaned tables. This spirit was originally thought to be one of the brothers, but it was later said to be one of the children who died in the house. Only recently reopened, investigations are beginning again at the River House.

The River House combines an old hotel and restaurant. The ballroom is known for its ghostly inhabitant. *Courtesy of author.*

Around the corner is a former Coyote Ugly Saloon. It was originally Lucky's Tavern, but it was not so lucky for several gangsters in the 1930s, who were gunned down inside the bar. Their grisly murders are still unsolved. Their spirits still inhabit the building, and people are frequently drawn by the sounds of shouting and gunfire, though the building is currently abandoned.

A short distance away, along the river, is the Stranahan House, which is another contender for the most haunted house in Florida. The Stranahan House was built in 1901 for Frank Stranahan and his wife, Ivy. Frank built the house near a location where he could run his ferry across the river. As the city seemed to grow around his home, Frank became the first postmaster of the New River Settlement. His home would also serve as a trading post, bank and even a makeshift town hall over the years.

Ivy was the settlement's first teacher. She held classes nearby but would host events on the upper floor of their house. The whole town began to use the second floor for dances and festivals. In 1906 Stranahan closed it to the public, and it became their private residence until Ivy passed away in 1971. Frank had died many years earlier, in June 1929. He had seen his businesses destroyed due to hurricanes and the Great Depression. He lost his own battle with depression and drowned himself off the dock behind his home. He tied himself to a large iron gate and jumped into the river. Reports of Frank's ghost began almost immediately, but he is not alone.

Six more family members died in the house. Ivy Cromartie Stranahan died in the upstairs bedroom. Witnesses say the scent of her perfume precedes her apparition. Her father, Augustus Cromartie, died in that same bedroom

Above: Lucky's Tavern was once the home of a Coyote Ugly Saloon. Now it sits empty, except for the ghosts. *Courtesy of author.*

Right: The Cooley Massacre memorial sits at the edge of Cooley's Landing Park. *Courtesy of author.*

years before his daughter and is said to haunt the room as well. The spirits of Ivy's brother and sister are said to often also haunt this location.

The final ghost is that of a Native American servant girl, who is seen here quite often. Her story is unknown, but she is seen so frequently that tours near the Stranahan house know to keep an eye out for her spirit.

The ghostly activity in the house has been reported many times. One homeless man sleeping near the house said that a lady in period garb chased him off the property by throwing rocks at him. Her description matched that of Ivy. Franks ghost is said to be in the museum, which is now housed on the first floor. He is known to touch visitors on the back and give them a wet and cold chill. Other ghostly sightings make this a dream destination for Florida ghost hunters.

The nearby Cooley's Landing Park is a memorial to the Cooley Massacre of the Second Seminole War. It is said to be haunted by the spirits of the Native Americans who were killed in vengeance for their attack on the Cooley ranch. These spirits move into the park at sunset and appear to try to plead their case, only to be shot by invisible defenders.

MIAMI

Long before Europeans arrived in South Florida, the Tequesta Indians lived and thrived in the land that now encompasses downtown Miami. The Miami Mystery Circle, which puzzled archaeologists for more than a decade, is now known to be where a community built their homes on stilts to avoid floods. The community thrived for hundreds of years.

The Spanish arrived in South Florida with Pedro Menendez de Aviles. They explored the area and left Jesuits to try to recruit the natives to the Catholic faith. They left for St. Augustine a short time later when they realized the native were not interested. The diseases the European settlers brought proved fatal to the tribe. There are no members of the Tequesta Indians still living today.

Cuba's first consul in Miami, Señor Pedro Don Domingo Milord, built a home for himself and his wife. They lived in the beautiful Villa Paula for six years before his wife became very ill. Her leg had swelled after being clawed by a diseased cat. It grew so infected in the Miami heat that it had to be amputated. She died from complications from the procedure.

Ever since her death, there have been paranormal events associated with the house. A strong smell of roses will arise in the building. Roses were brought in to hide the smell of her diseased leg. Some visitors smell Cuban coffee brewing in the kitchen even though it is abandoned. The most heinous occurrence, though, is that the gate outside often slams shut. When passing feral cats wander close to the house, the iron gate slams shut and kills countless stray cats. Is it Señor Pedro Don Domingo Milord or his wife who is angered by the feline visitors?

The Villa Paula is currently seeking a new buyer. *Courtesy of author.*

The oldest cemetery in the Miami is Pinewood Cemetery, which was once known as the Cocuplum Cemtery. There are gravestones here dating back as early as 1855. No one knows how many people are buried in this small cemetery. Two hurricanes and improper recordkeeping make tracking the dead here quite complicated. Some believe more than three hundred people are buried here, but there are very few stones. Others believe the number is actually quite higher.

Paranormal investigators frequent the cemetery due to the large assortment of paranormal activity. From echoing footsteps to guttural growls, the recordings taken here are quite impressive. There are even reports of full-body apparitions.

The thing to lookout for is a strange, white mist that seems to float against the wind in the cemetery. Some visitors feel a strange chill when it is near, despite the omnipresent tropical heat. Photographs of the mist seem to show shapes of gaunt figures within.

Nearby, in Coral Gables, is the most famous haunted location in the Miami area: the glamorous Biltmore Hotel. It opened in 1926 and was one of the greatest events of its age. "Miami Biltmore Special" trains even came straight to the hotel. The trains brought tourists from all over the northeast to the new crown jewel of South Florida.

The designer of the hotel also designed the whole area of Coral Gables for the affluent. His name was George E. Merrick. Merrick sought out investor and hotelier John Bowman, who accepted his offer to build and finance the Biltmore.

Huge columns and marble floors line the halls of the Biltmore. Carved woodwork rises up to the painted ceilings. You also can't miss the large swimming pool outside. It was once the largest in the world and is still the largest in the United States. At its peak, it hosted polo matches, gondola rides, beauty pageants and even the World Championships swim meet. The grounds of the hotel even held annual fox hunts.

Even though the '20s and '30s brought the Great Depression, the Biltmore seemed to rise above it. Its giant tower seemed to loom over everything. The hotel continued to host wealthy and famous guests, who were drawn in by big band concerts, golf tournaments, aquatic shows and even alligator wrestling.

The pool's swimming instructor was Johnny Weissmuller. His physique earned him notice from a few of the Hollywood elite who vacationed at the hotel. It would help land him the part of Tarzan, which filmed in Silver Springs, Florida.

In the late 1920s, during Prohibition, the hotel hosted an illegal speakeasy on the thirteenth floor. This was usually home to visiting gangsters from the North. The speakeasy had gambling and alcohol, so there was plenty to keep them occupied.

In 1928 Thomas "Fatty" Walsh murdered one of his gang members in New York. He fled to Florida and wound up in Miami at the Biltmore. Fatty ran the speakeasy with gambler Ed Wilson. They ran the place for more than a year, and business was good. Wilson noted that the gambling was making more money than the alcohol. He pressed Fatty for a larger percentage of the earnings. In a room full of witnesses, Walsh shot Fatty twice during the argument. When the police arrived, the elevator was apparently out of service. They police had to climb the stairs to the thirteenth floor. What they

Rose Cemetery is so small that it sits between a CVS and a busy four-lane road. *Courtesy of author.*

didn't know was that all of the people in the speakeasy fled via the elevator while they were climbing up the stairs.

The records of this are reported as missing by the City of Miami. Apparently, several city officials were in the speakeasy at the time as regulars. Other prominent members of the community were frequent visitors of the club. Fatty's murderer was neither arrested nor prosecuted.

Fatty's ghost is seen often on the thirteenth floor. He is often seen with an unknown blonde woman in flapper attire. His cigar smoke fills the room, and a cool wind blows it around the room. The couple are often heard with her giggling and him laughing loudly.

Employees and guests say Fatty likes to bring people on the elevator to his place on the thirteenth floor, whether they intended to go there or not. He famously pulled a lady and her husband up to the room. They had tried to go to the fourth floor, but the elevator went all the way up. The doors to the elevator stayed open for several minutes while they were trying to go back down. When the wife stepped out, the doors quickly closed and sent the elevator back to the fourth floor.

The husband raced to the lobby and got the hotel staff to override the elevator and go to the thirteenth floor as quickly as he could. He found his wife in hysterics. She was terrified of the tall, dark man who had threatened her. The smell of cigar smoke surrounded them.

The most famous incident on the thirteenth floor involves President Bill Clinton. He was staying at the hotel and planned to watch a football game in the main room on the thirteenth floor with his staff. The lights and television began to turn themselves on and off. The president insisted that his staff move to another room to watch the game.

During World War II, the Biltmore, like so many other hotels in Florida, was commandeered by the army as a hospital facility. Many wounded soldiers died within the walls of the grand hotel. Another ghost seen at the hotel is that of a nurse in white jumping from the top floor of the tower, though there are no records of any such incident happening.

The hotel sat abandoned for many years, mostly in the '70s and early '80s. Urban explorers loved coming to the building. Many heard the sounds of music and saw soldiers in the abandoned halls. Some people even spoke of Fatty and his lady way up on the thirteenth floor. Today, the hotel has been restored to its former glory and is a beautiful place to visit. The pool is still a must see. Just make sure that if you go to the thirteenth floor, you're ready to meet the ghost of a notorious killer.

KEY WEST

Key West is known for its eclectic history and esoteric citizens. Once, the entire city rebelled against the United States and declared itself "The Conch Republic." A few minutes later, they surrendered and demanded $8 billion in foreign aid. The town is known as Cayo Hueso, which means "the key of bones" in English. The local Native Americans used the town as their burial grounds.

One of the oldest saloons in Florida is located in Key West. It used to be the famous Sloppy Joe's that Ernest Hemingway frequented. Captain Tony's has several remarkable features—the first is the fish outside. It is said that if you flip a quarter into the mouth of the fish, you will have luck for the rest of the week.

Inside, you will see a giant tree growing right in the middle of the bar. This tree was once the town hanging tree, and dozens of documented executions occurred on it. At the base of the tree is a tombstone. The building once served as an icehouse and then a morgue, and there are several tombstones here.

Where the pool tables are today, there is a tombstone that reads "Elvira, daughter of Joseph and Susannah Edmunds. Died Dec. 21, 1822 Age 19 Years, 8 months and 21 days." There are several rumors that Elvira was a witch and was hanged on the tree. Other stories say she was one of the lovers of a condemned man and killed herself to be buried next to him. The witch story seems to come from her sharing the name of the famous horror host Elvira, Mistress of the Dark, because there are no records of that legend before the late 1980s.

Left: One of the graves at the base of the hanging tree in what is now Captain Tony's Saloon. *Courtesy of author.*

Below: The Hemingway House is a popular tourist spot in Key West. *Courtesy of author.*

The other tombstone belongs to a woman named Reba Sawyer. She supposedly had an affair with a married man at the bar. When her aggrieved husband found out about the affair after her death, he dragged the tombstone to the sidewalk outside of Captain Tony's. The captain himself saw an opportunity and dragged the stone inside.

One of these women's ghosts may haunt the ladies' room. Women often report seeing the strange, scary face of a woman standing behind them in the mirror. The woman seems to be screaming but cannot be heard. When they turn around, she vanishes. Some say there is the smell of death and decay in the air just after she makes her startling appearance.

Speaking of Hemingway, his house is a must-see for most tourists. Many claims have been reported of seeing him waving from upper windows as witnesses pass by the home. Docents in his home also claim to hear the sounds of his typewriter echoing through the halls. There is a contest for Hemingway look-alikes every year, which could explain the happy waving of the often-reclusive author.

The most famous residents of the house are the six-toed cats. The house still hosts dozens of the descendants of Hemingway's cats. Many have six toes on their paws. The docents, though, claim to see many of the same cats months after they have died. Paranormal pets are not a new phenomenon—ghosts of dogs and cats are quite commonly sighted. Keep a watchful eye on the six-toed cats here.

Marrero's Guest Mansion is a beautiful hotel that was once the home of famous cigar maker Francisco Marrero. It was built in 1889, when Key West was one of the wealthiest cities in America. Marrero built the house for his wife, Enriquetta. After a few short years, Francisco died while on a business trip back to Cuba.

Enriquetta was sad, but she and her children had the large house where they could continue to live. Then a woman from Cuba came to Key West. She claimed to be the first wife of Francisco Marrero. They had never divorced. This meant his marriage to Enriquetta was not legal. His first wife claimed the house as her own, and the courts backed her. Enriquetta and her eight children were forced to leave their home. Their story ends here, and no one is quite sure what happened to them after this. Those who visit the mansion say that Enriquetta and her children never left.

Rooms 17, 19 and 23 seem to be a hotbed of paranormal encounters. The children can be heard running through the halls, and Enriquetta's scolding in Spanish is heard shortly thereafter. Several guests in room 23

Be careful of what you'll see in the bathroom mirror at Captain Tony's Saloon. *Illustration by Kari Schultz.*

have seen a woman who fits the description of Enriquetta staring out of the window in the room late at night.

The Artist's House is famous because it was the longtime home of Robert the Haunted Doll. Key West's most infamous resident is now in the Fort East Martello Museum across town. We discussed his amazing story in *Eerie Florida*. Needless to say, the most haunted doll in the world is a story worth delving further into.

The house has its own haunted history that may have influenced the possession of Robert the Doll. Built in the 1890s by famous painter Robert Eugene Otto and his wife and talented pianist, Anne, the house rivals the Hemingway House as the most photographed building in Key West, thanks to its Colonial style and many columns and verandas. The most visually stunning part of the building is the turret.

The turret room was the home of Robert the Doll, when young Robert Eugene O'Neil, a later resident, began to misbehave and blamed it on his

The Curry Mansion Inn was the home of a tragic suicide by the son of the original owner. When he lost all of his family's money, he decided to take his own life. His ghost still lingers in the lobby of the beautiful hotel. *Courtesy of author.*

doll. Recent investigations into the Artist's House have added a wrinkle to that infamous legend. They suggest Robert wasn't always haunted. One of the more malevolent spirits in the house used the doll to make its escape.

Guests have reported seeing a lady in a long, flowing wedding gown descending the stairs quietly from the turret room. As she approaches, her appearance grows even more lovely and beautiful. Witnesses say she looks like Anne Otto. When she reaches the side of the bed, she vanishes and leaves the smell of roses.

The other presence here is much darker and may be tied to Robert. Mediums have claimed that the dark presence is not a human ghost. They claim it is an elemental negative spirit that lives on fear. It sends the ghost of Anne to awaken guests and make them curious. When they begin to stir and look for the ghost, it strikes with a sudden forceful shove.

Once back on the bed, the shadow shape climbs on top of the victims and holds them down, trapping them under a tremendous weight. Some have even spoken of the feeling of being strangled. When the level of fear reaches its peak, the entity is satiated and dissipates, leaving the area cold.

The employees of the Artist's House love to talk about Robert and Anne but will quickly shush any talk of the dark spirit. Paranormal investigators in the city of Key West, though, have documented the spirit many times over

The graves of those who died in the famous disaster that started the Spanish-American War. "Remember the Maine!" *Courtesy of author.*

the years. The entity seems to be more active in the fall and winter months, but that may be because it is a busier season for visitors.

Guarding the port is old Fort Zachary Taylor. It was built in 1845, after the War of 1812 led to a massive building effort to defend the ports of the United States. Between the fort and the two batteries of East and West Martello, the port of Key West was well defended indeed.

Held by the Union during the Civil War, the fort buried its cannons and replaced them with new artillery for the Spanish-American War and again during both world wars and the Cuban Missile Crisis, before finally becoming a national park.

One of the soldiers here is called Wendall. Wendall is known to walk the halls of Fort Zach, as the locals call it. The ghost is often seen on the stairwells and walking through walled-in additions to the rooms that came from later periods. Wendall will often stop and ask tourists if they are allowed to be in certain rooms. Many believe him to be some reenactor, which leads to interesting talks with the park rangers.

Other noted sites in Key West include the Key West Cemetery, which has several ghostly women who mourn at the site of the memorial of the USS *Maine*, which was destroyed at the start of the Spanish-American War. These women may be the ghosts of the wives of the lost sailors. The cemetery houses many other spirits with echoing footsteps and even laughing children.

IN CONCLUSION

While no one can tell you if ghosts are real or not, many will try to argue their point one way or the other. We enjoy calling the supernatural the preternatural—we just don't understand the rules yet. Many emerging sciences and medicinal treatments would have been laughed out of universities just a few decades ago. Perhaps one day, parapsychology can also count itself as one of those emerging sciences we finally figure out.

While we do discount some stories in this book, we try to leave everything on the table. There are so many witnesses and documents to tie these encounters together. People do see and experience unusual things. We have three books full of their stories—there simply must be something to all of them.

Lastly, we've noticed that many on the fringe sciences don't seem to like each other's fields. Ghost hunters often scoff at UFO researchers. Bigfoot hunters seem to hate psychics and mediums. It seems so odd to us when we are all in this together. Try to be nice to your fellow preternatural investigators and enthusiasts. Some bridges have been forming recently, and it is good to see.

Kari and I tied the knot just before this book went to publication. We've been around this state several times and keep finding more stories. Will we ever cross the Georgia border? We certainly hope so. This is our third book with The History Press, and we are very proud of them. We hope you have enjoyed all of them.

We love seeing all our readers and fans at the many conventions and book signings we do every year. Keep an eye on EerieFlorida.com to see where we're turning up next. We're always thrilled to see those of you who have checkmarks and tabs for the places you've traveled in our books.

We'll see you on the other side,

MARK MUNCY AND KARI SCHULTZ

Opposite: Kari Schultz and Mark Muncy of *Creepy Florida. Courtesy of Heather Richchi-Blocker.*

ABOUT THE AUTHOR
AND ILLUSTRATOR

MARK MUNCY is the creator of Hellview Cemetery, a charity haunted house in Central Florida that was so infamous it was banned by the City of St. Petersburg. An author of horror and science fiction, he has spent more than three decades collecting ghostly tales and reports of legendary beasts. This is his third book for The History Press after the successful *Eerie Florida* and *Freaky Florida*. He lives in St. Petersburg, Florida, on the remains of an ancient midden with his wife, Kari Schultz. Occasionally, he is visited by his daughters when they remember he is still there.

KARI SCHULTZ is a varied illustrator at Fox Dream Studio, who enjoys fantasy and horror. She has been working on art as long as she can remember and reading folklore and horror almost as long. This is her fourth work for The History Press, as she ventured into another state with *Eerie Alabama*. She has a thing for foxes. When not drawing, she is the caretaker of her baby dragon named Clawdius and her miniature giant space serpent called Missy. She can be lured forth from her home with sushi or pasta.

Visit us at
www.historypress.com